LIGHT *the* NIGHT

Preserve Hickory
Traverse City, Michigan

Copyright © 2011 Preserve Hickory

All rights reserved.

Published by Preserve Hickory, Traverse City, Michigan
www.preservehickory.com

Publisher's Cataloging-in-Publication Data

Tompkins, Molly.
    Light the night : a history of Hickory Hills / Molly Tompkins and Ryan Ness.
       p. cm.
    ISBN: 978-0-615-53837-2
    1. Traverse City (Mich.)—History. 2. Grand Traverse region,
Mich.—History.   I. Ness, Ryan. II. Title.
F572.G5 T66 2011
977.4`64—dc22

                                                                             2011917077

Printed in Canada

Design by Tarra Dalley Warnes

15 14 13 12 11   *   5 4 3 2 1

First Edition

All proceeds from this book go to Preserve Hickory, a nonprofit organization, to ensure that Hickory remains true to its original mission.

SIMPLE GIFT, RICH RETURN

In April 2010, our moms asked us to join them at a breakfast meeting. Although we were high school sophomores who both grew up skiing at Hickory, we really didn't know each other well. A breakfast meeting seemed a bit weird, but we're always looking for free food and were intrigued by the invitation. We agreed to go.

Moms have a special knack for making jobs sound easy. Their pitch was smooth: "Would you be willing to write a short history of our local ski hill, Hickory?" After listening a while, we figured the task would be relatively simple — take a few photos, do a little research, dig up some facts and maybe interview a few family friends about their own Hickory ski experiences. No big deal, right?

Our first interview had a strong impact. Larry Bensley, the son of Hickory's visionary, Loren Bensley, opened our eyes to Hickory's rich history. Larry spoke eloquently about his father's vision for an affordable ski area in Traverse City and about meeting his own wife of more than fifty years while skiing under Hickory's "romantic" lights. His eyes sparkled as he shared memories, and his excitement for the project inspired us. Larry also suggested we seek donations for the book's publication so we could donate all of its sales proceeds back to Hickory Hills. From that first interview, our project evolved from a seemingly simple historical documentation to a community-wide volunteer effort that has taken nearly two years to complete.

At first, our research consisted of days spent sifting through old microfiche news articles and photos — we were overwhelmed. We were uneasy and didn't really know how to proceed. Luckily, early support from the Traverse City *Record-Eagle* helped get word out about the book. Testimonials and memories of Hickory flooded in from all over the country — through e-mails, blog entries and phone calls. Hickory Hills veterans pulled dusty shoeboxes full of forgotten mementos out of their closets and basements. People poured out their hearts, re-creating for us a sense of the magic they had experienced at Hickory.

At times, the work seemed endless. We pulled all-nighters in ski team hotel rooms. We made phone calls while traveling across Michigan for cross-country and debate competitions. We often conducted three interviews a day —between ACT preparation and studying for finals. And just when we felt exhausted or discouraged, we would be rejuvenated by calls like one from a seventy-year-old skier in Colorado who still has her very first Grand Traverse Ski Club race bib hanging in her living room. We felt compelled to share the stories of so many who took the time to speak with us, who shed real tears of joy in the retelling.

After more than seventy interviews, we've learned that history is best expressed through stories — real voices describing real experiences. And as we've become immersed in these stories, Hickory's history has become more than just one more obligation for two busy high school juniors — the story is a part of us. Hickory has meant the world to so many people. And knowing they're depending on us to share their stories has compelled us to keep going and never give up.

To all those who inspired and encouraged us — sharing emotions and recalling memories of Hickory — we present to you: *Light the Night.* This small history captures the memories of hundreds like you who also love Hickory Hills.

And while words can speak volumes, we also know pictures can shout. *Light the Night* could never have captured the essence of our little hill without the stunning photographs of local photographer Jack Bensley. The Bensley family's generosity in allowing us to see Hickory through the eyes of young Jack Bensley gave us a clear vision: the book had to revolve around his images. It just felt right.

We chose the title *Light the Night* to reflect what we've heard over and over: Hickory has been a beacon of light through dark northern Michigan winters that offers affordable and safe recreation to all youth. Consistent with the spirit of giving that is the foundation of Hickory's history, all the expenses and publication costs of *Light the Night* have been paid through the financial support of our gracious donors. Their generosity also makes it possible for us to dedicate all sales proceeds from *Light the Night* to the Preserve Hickory organization, ensuring that future generations will have an opportunity to forge their own unforgettable memories at our tiny but mighty city-owned ski hill.

We knew Hickory Hills contributed significantly to Traverse City's heritage, but through the process of writing this book, we have come to realize its history is richer than we ever imagined. Little did we know that saying yes to a simple request from our moms would provide such a rich return — to our community, to Hickory and to us.

Molly Tompkins and Ryan Ness, Fall 2011

MIND, BODY AND SOUL

Hickory Hills is more than a small local ski area with tow ropes. It was, and is, a special world of friends, of adults who care, of lessons to be learned and the embodiment of a "can-do" community that set the stage for my future.

Memories of ski crashes, snow down my neck, below-zero nights and, yes, childhood romance play in my head. I can hear the PA system blasting out the old *Piano Roll Blues* and echoing through the crisp night air. At the bottom of Buck you could escape the frigid cold and enter the warmth of the cozy lodge. A crackling open fireplace, the smell of fresh chili and the camaraderie of good friends.

Hickory Hills has always permeated my mind, body and soul.

Hickory skier Dick Swan
Traverse City Senior High School '61

CONTENTS

FOREWORD..XV

INTRODUCTION...XIX

one HUMBLE HILL, BIG VISION..1
One Man's Vision
Ci-Bo Hill
Hickory Hills
The Early Years

two EMERGING SPORT, LEGENDARY LEADER.................43
A Born Leader
Becoming American: The 10th Mountain Division
Talent Travels to Traverse City
A Public School Ski School
A Leader of Athletes

three SMALL TOWN, BIG WORLD......................................53
A Small Town Embraces a New Sport
Learning the Ropes

four PINT-SIZED CLUB, HUGE IMPROVEMENTS...............85
Racer Ready?
Race Clinics
Bridging the Gap
Give a Little, Get a Lot

five LITTLE RACERS, FULL SPEED..................................125
A Legacy of Top Racers
It's Official
Hickory Racers Hit the Big Time
Hickory Racers Come Home

six FLEETING MOMENTS, LASTING MEMORIES...............159
The Trek to the Hill
The Ropes
The Face of Pete
The Lodge
Shenanigans
Broken Skis, Broken Bones
Romance

NARROW LENS, WIDE VIEW..186

THE MAGIC OF LIGHTED SLOPES..................................188

ACKNOWLEDGEMENTS...190

SOURCES..192

DONORS...194

HICKORY'S STATE CHAMPIONS.....................................195

PHOTO CREDITS AND IDENTIFICATION........................196

THE AUTHORS..201

FOREWORD

In this book, you'll find a very old photograph of me from sometime in the mid-1950s. I'm six, maybe seven. I'm wearing a very flat brimmed hat with earflaps, a toothy grin and the number twelve. My father, Hans "Peppi" Teichner, a key figure in the story told here, is handing me a Hickory Hills patch, which I still have.

The picture has a backstory. There are other photographs to prove it. I had just completed a race, and as far as I can recall, I came in last. I had skied down the hill in a perfectly controlled snowplow, as slowly as a skier could possibly ski and still be moving. The other photographs show bystanders cheering me on, no doubt calling out, "Faster, faster!" But I didn't get it — I failed to comprehend that going fast was the point.

Some fathers would have been irritated and berated their children for showing no competitive spirit whatsoever — not mine, even though my misguided effort might have been seen as an embarrassment to a skier and coach of his caliber and reputation. My father smiled and rewarded me with my treasured Hickory Hills patch.

He cared that I was having fun and that I loved skiing, not whether I was a future Olympian. Instead of subjecting me to the pressure of being the pro's daughter, he enrolled me in the Record-Eagle Ski School just like all the other kids — to become a racer or not.

Hickory Hills symbolizes what my father believed America was all about. Forced by oppression and war to leave two countries, first Germany and then Spain, he believed skiing saved his life. He survived and managed to reach the United States because he was a famous skier, whose wealthy skier friends got him out. Once here, he gloried in democracy. He helped create Hickory Hills in the image of his ideal — a joyful place where everyone could ski, not just the rich. A place where instruction and equipment were available so any kid with talent and ambition could become a champion.

Peppi Teichner loved the fact that skiing quickly became a way of life in Traverse City. It was something easy for a family to do together, on weekends or possibly after dinner, because even in the 1950s, the slopes at Hickory Hills were lit at night. My father used to laugh when the weatherman on WPBN-TV did the weather in ski clothes, because he either was going to Hickory Hills after the broadcast or had just returned.

Then, as now, there were only rope tows. If you were little, as I was when the picture was taken, the rope was too heavy to pick up. Because it was moving, it dug deep grooves in the snow, which always ended up ice. So kids crowded around the spot where adults got on and watched. The instant someone large came along, hauled the rope up and tightened his or her grasp on it, some little goggle-clad creature scrambled into place right behind and hung on for dear life all the way up the hill. I may not have been very good at racing, but I was an expert rope tow grabber and absolutely fearless. What I remember most is the sublime feeling of freedom I had, because I had the run of the place. It was small enough and safe enough so that was possible, and I loved every second I spent there.

I know my father would be very pleased and proud that Hickory Hills still exists. The fact that it continues to successfully do what he believed it was meant to do is pretty amazing. Actually, it has continued for more than half a century now, thanks to hundreds of believers. You've got to give them credit. Think about the name Hickory Hills. Hills, not mountains, in an age when bigger always seems to be better, cooler. Somehow the people who've kept Hickory going have done more than make sure the lights are on at night or the rope tows are working. With their enthusiasm and hard work, they've passed along the wonder of skiing intact.

Martha Teichner
New York, New York
July 2011

Martha Teichner is the daughter of Hickory legend Peppi Teichner. She was born in Traverse City and lived in northern Michigan until the age of nine. She graduated from Wellesley College in 1969 with a bachelor's degree in economics. Teichner also attended the University of Chicago's Graduate School of Business Administration. A national correspondent for CBS News and a senior correspondent for CBS News Sunday Morning, she lives in New York. Her work has been recognized with three Emmy Awards, for reports on Princess Diana's death, the Detroit newspaper strike and a factory workers' lawsuit against the Maytag Company. Teichner also interviewed First Lady Hillary Rodham Clinton for Sunday Morning in 1995 and 1997.

INTRODUCTION

At the forty-fifth parallel, tucked into the pinky of northern Michigan's Lower Peninsula, lies a mid-twentieth-century homegrown ski area. Eight short trails among the trees, just five tow ropes, a shed-style lodge, hand-hewn ski racks and woodpiles. Hickory Hills measures less than one-fifth of a square mile and boasts only 230 feet of vertical.

Tiny in terrain, Hickory is larger than life. Imagined by one man with vision, the small ski park emerged from the woods through the persistence, hard work and collaboration of Traverse City–area civic leaders and businesses. Hickory's lights started to shine in 1952 through dark, bitterly cold winter nights, drawing children and families out from their homes and into a new community — skiers.

Hickory has not only survived the test of time but also remained frozen in time, physically and philosophically. Just as its founding fathers envisioned, Hickory remains a community ski hill — a public park with accessible and affordable skiing for everyone to enjoy.

Hickory is a small hill with a big story: a tale of vision, hard work, passion and love — old themes that never go out of style.

LIGHT *the* NIGHT

one

HUMBLE HILL, BIG VISION

It was the jewel of the north.

Rosie Hutchison

Ci-Bo started as the dream of one man. It blossomed into a full community effort.

Traverse City *Record-Eagle*, December 1950

ONE MAN'S VISION

Loren Bensley, a savvy Traverse City politician and business owner, had vision. Big vision. Drawing inspiration from a news article describing Howelsen Hill, a small city-operated ski hill in Steamboat Springs, Colorado, Bensley believed, "We can do that." And with the good will, generosity and help of others, that's exactly what they did.

CI-BO HILL

Bensley's vision became a reality when Traverse City's commissioners established a joint recreation committee with the local school district. Based on Bensley's recommendation, the committee set out to develop Traverse City's first ski hill.

What was once called Rennie Hill — a gentle slope, a natural bowl scooped from the hillside — and owned by the Traverse City school district, the site appeared to be an ideal location for a ski hill. Sitting on a high plateau at the city's south limits, the land had once been the Traverse City airport and was already cleared. Bensley and John Norton, one of Boyne Mountain's original partners, asked School Superintendent Glenn Loomis for permission to borrow the property. Loomis lent them Rennie Hill and dedicated funds to the project on behalf of the school board. After donations from the city, the school district and area businesses had been made, construction of Ci-Bo Hill — named for the city ("Ci") and board of education ("Bo") partnership — began in November 1950.

City workers installed a single tow rope, powered by a ten-horsepower electric motor. Cone Drive donated custom-designed gears. Traverse City Iron Works supplied the pulleys. Wheels came from Heights Auto Parts in Muskegon, and local lumber dealers donated construction materials for a warming hut. With that collaborative manpower, Ci-Bo opened for business in December 1950. Ci-Bo utilized lights installed by Traverse City Light and Power — becoming the first ski area in Michigan to offer night skiing.

Although hundreds of youngsters and adults flocked to Ci-Bo, very few knew how to ski. Bensley recognized that

Ci-Bo was located just south of the intersection of Division Street and 14th Street on the east side of the highway.

"you couldn't just step on the boards; you had to learn how to stop and turn." He also discovered that other towns had convinced newspapers and local service organizations to sponsor ski schools. With the help of Peppi Teichner, an experienced German ski instructor new to the area, Bensley pitched the concept to the Traverse City *Record-Eagle*. In December 1950 for five consecutive Saturdays, the first Record-Eagle Ski School operated under the leadership of Teichner and several volunteer instructors.

But with only two runs — one beginner and one more difficult — Ci-Bo could not keep pace with skier demand. More space was needed after only one season.

THE FATHER OF TRAVERSE CITY SKIING

Loren Bensley had two local passions: area youth and the future of skiing.

Bensley masterminded the opening of Traverse City's first ski hill, Ci-Bo. He not only generated support among those who translated his dream into a snow-covered hill and working tow rope but also fueled excitement about the sport within the community. When Ci-Bo outgrew its capacity in its first year, Bensley transferred his enthusiasm and extraordinary leadership into a bigger, better and more permanent home for skiers: Hickory Hills. He always knew "we could do it."

Because he worked tirelessly to carry out his vision of a small publicly owned and supported ski hill where youth could ski for free, in 1959 Bensley was honored with the award of Traverse City Citizen of the Year. He was inducted posthumously into the Grand Traverse Ski Club's Hall of Fame in 2008. Without Loren Bensley — the "Father of Traverse City Skiing" — locals might still be hibernating during the winter.

HICKORY HILLS

So began the hunt for new land.

Gerald "Buck" Williams, then director of Traverse City Parks and Recreation, took up the search. Williams didn't have to look beyond his family. His brother-in-law, Lud Garthe, a city commissioner himself, owned a wooded tract of land intimately familiar to Williams. A hiking and hunting destination that boasted beautiful views of the west arm of Grand Traverse Bay, the seventeen-acre plot was untouched yet close to town. Garthe didn't need much convincing. Born with a clubfoot and unable to ski himself, he believed in recreation for kids. Garthe leased his land to the city for just one dollar a year.

John Norton, Boyne Mountain partner and Ci-Bo trail designer, went to work designing Hickory's hills. Garthe's land provided enough ground for five runs — one black diamond, one beginner and three intermediate slopes. Christened "Hickory Hills," the ski area was named for the hard hickory wood then used to make downhill skis.

Inmates from the Grand Traverse County jail cut the trails from the trees. City engineers and employees spooled more than two thousand feet of Columbian rope through pulleys — Hickory's tow ropes. Volunteering his services, local

one: Humble Hill, Big Vision

architect Orus Eash designed a shed-roof lodge — more than fourteen hundred square feet of snack bar, lounge and fireplace. With donated materials, skilled laborers laid the foundation and built the structure. Volunteers brought their own brushes and tools to a November 1951 work bee. The lodge was built in just ninety days.

Hickory Hills Ski Lodge

ORUS EASH — ARCHITECT

Finally, the lights. Cherryland Electric Cooperative powered Hickory Hill's first lights — lights that would illuminate dark winter nights in Traverse City. On January 3, 1952, Hickory turned on the lights, started the ropes and lit a fire in the lodge.

hickory
hills

HICKORY'S ORIGINAL LOGO

Hickory Hills was named for a 1950s classic — the "hickory boards that took you down the hill," remembers Larry Bensley, who was seventeen when Hickory opened. Those skis were long. Bensley's first pair measured as tall as his palm stretched high over his head.

Designed by Geraldine Cowell in 1951, Hickory's original logo incorporated an image of a pair of upright hickory skis embellished with hickory leaves. Cowell and her husband, Wayne, volunteered at Hickory's Sunday races. Their daughters, Sue and Joey, raced for the Hickory Hills Ski Club and Traverse City Senior High School. A Traverse City resident, Cowell studied interior design at the University of Michigan. She engaged in various artistic pursuits throughout her life.

Ci-Bo Hill was a great beginning for skiing, but we thought we were really livin' when Hickory opened.

Barb Sherberneau Loveland

It was a gathering place. Hickory brought families together and built friendships.

Carl Madion

one: Humble Hill, Big Vision   21

PETE would do anything for Traverse City. He was a great man.

Fran Batsakis

SWEDE was bound and determined to have a hill for the local kids. He worked really hard to get the city on board.

Clayton "Swede" Johnson Jr.

BUCK was a good man to respect. You couldn't get a more friendly or knowledgeable guy in Traverse City. Everybody enjoyed him.

Bob Fifarek

JACK was devoted to the community and the schools. He was a leader; people trusted and looked up to him.

Paul Hazelton

THE TRAILBLAZERS*

Hickory's trails were named for the men who were instrumental in Hickory's development. Buck for Buck Williams. Pete for Pete Batsakis. Jack's Trail for Jack Bensley. Swede for Swede Johnson.

*While some credit trail dedication to Pete Rennie and Jack Merrill, both significant contributors to Hickory, the majority of sources credit others.

Hickory's steepest hill and most daunting black diamond: Pete. Tucked between Hickory's peak and the lodge at its base, Pete is short and steep — named in honor of Pete Batsakis Sr., a highly respected businessman and owner of several local restaurants, including the U&I Lounge, Pete's Café and the Batsakis Inn. Known for his generous hospitality, Batsakis was one of the earliest financial contributors to Hickory Hills. Fran Batsakis remembers that "no kid ever walked out of Pete's Café without a lollipop." A savvy fundraiser with a solid commitment to the vision for Hickory Hills, Batsakis hosted the first Hickory Hills Ski Club benefit dinner in 1952 at the Batsakis Inn. The event became a tradition for the ski club — the club's annual steak fry.

Buck, one of Hickory's beloved blue trails, is Hickory's most popular trail. Named after Gerald "Buck" Williams, former Traverse City Parks and Recreation superintendent and a civic leader for forty-four years, the hill draws intermediate skiers and racers moving up to more advanced age groups. Having hunted and hiked the Hickory property as a young man, Williams and his intimacy with the land proved instrumental in the selection of Hickory's location.

As the Parks and Recreation superintendent, Williams assigned only those city employees to Hickory who worked well with children and families. While considered by many as a "no-nonsense kind of guy," Williams held a reputation as a fair and respected leader. "If you did your job right, he was behind you one hundred percent," remembers Larry Bensley.

Hickory's longest hill, dedicated in 1956, overlooks the city of Traverse City with broad territorial views of the west arm of Grand Traverse Bay. The trail was named in honor of Oscar "Swede" Johnson, a Traverse City city commissioner and owner of Swede's, a local Plymouth and Chrysler auto dealership. The slope is Hickory's most interesting, served by two tow ropes and bordered by trees on both sides. Johnson had a passion for public and youth recreation and pioneered Hickory as a city-owned park. He generously donated personal time and resources to ensure Hickory's completion and success. During Hickory's development, Johnson often stopped by Hickory to help with construction after his workday. He remained a valuable advocate until his death in 1955.

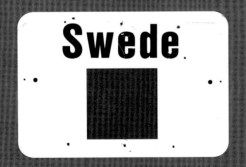

A favorite "more difficult" slope that meanders through Hickory's woods, Jack's Trail was named for Jack Bensley. A natural competitor and athlete, Bensley was a member of Traverse City High School's state championship basketball team, as well as the football and tennis teams, from 1938 through 1941. Out of love for children and sports, Bensley made his mark on Hickory when he conceived of and organized the Grand Traverse Ski Club's junior racing program.

Bensley envisioned Hickory's Sunday races as a feeder system: if the ski club could produce youth racers, then high school teams would be more competitive. Bensley was right. Hickory's racing program is one of a kind, still producing many of Michigan's best high school racers.

"Jack was a rooter for Traverse City. He was one of the early pioneers of skiing here," recalls Sandy Blumenfeld.

THE EARLY YEARS

Over the next decade, Hickory grew. With labor provided by a crew of prison inmates from the Michigan Department of Corrections work camp program based out of Camp Lehman near Grayling, the city cleared more trees and added the Upper Birch Run in 1952. The following season, inmates erected split-rail fences combined with pine seedlings to separate the trails, constructed two new tows, built a pump house and dry well and erected lighting on Pete. They also constucted a dam on the small creek near the lodge to provide a skating rink. In 1956, the city installed two additional tow ropes to serve its new and longest trail, Swede. One year later, municipal workers widened the slopes to accommodate more skiers and enhance skier safety. They graded and graveled Hickory's entrance road and improved the parking lot. In 1959, the lodge grew with the addition of a ski patrol room, dedicated to Jack Merrill.

Hiking trails and nature lured nonskiers to enjoy the public park year-round. Hickory even served as one of Michigan's first summer camps for disabled children, Camp Roy-El.

THE LAND GRAB

The City of Traverse City acquired seven privately owned lots covering more than 125 acres to develop Hickory. Over a thirty-year span and for a total purchase price of $59,638, a large, hilly tract of land became a public ski park.

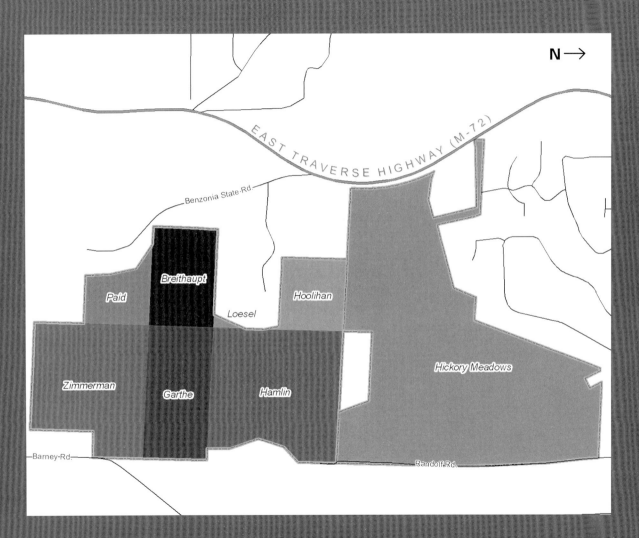

1951 Hickory's first stake in the ground was on the Garthe lot. Owned by Lud and Dorothy Garthe, it became the heart of the public park. Hickory's lodge and trails Pete, Buck and Birch sit squarely on this land. In 1951, Lud Garthe agreed to lease the original seventeen-acre parcel to the city for just $1 a year in response to a request from his brother-in-law, Buck Williams. After her husband's death, Dorothy Garthe sold the Garthe lot to the city in 1968 for $5,000 — the cost of her tax obligation.

1954 For just $1, Ronald Breithaupt transferred a parcel to the city equal in size and adjacent to the Garthe lot. This generous gift became the beautiful back hills of Hickory and home to Hickory's longest run, Swede.

1955 The city leased from Max Hamlin the lot directly north and adjacent to the original Garthe lot. This parcel provided direct access from Hickory to city streets and became the location of the entrance and parking lot. In 1974, the city was able to purchase the property with state recreation bond funds for $26,625.

1955–1969 Hickory lived within these three original parcels (just thirty-two acres) for thirty years but regularly borrowed an additional seventy acres through very loose lease arrangements.

1970 The state of Michigan issued $100 million in recreation bonds, $30 million of which was earmarked for local government. Traverse City submitted a recreation proposal for comprehensive improvements to the Hickory Hills Recreation Center. It envisioned a multipurpose winter recreation center to include tobogganing, sledding, Nordic skiing, hiking and snowshoe trails and even a ski jump. It was the city's "number one priority" and was expected to "meet the recreation needs for the greatest number of people in the community and the area." With the recreation bond monies it received, the city purchased five lots for Hickory Hills.

1971 The city bought the Zimmerman lot, directly south of the Garthe lot, for $16,500.

1972 For $4,145, the city purchased the Paid lot.

1972 With $6,500 in bond funds, the city acquired the Hoolihan lot, adjacent to Hickory Meadows.

1975 The Loesel lot, a small triangle lot behind Hickory's lodge, became a part of Hickory for $867.

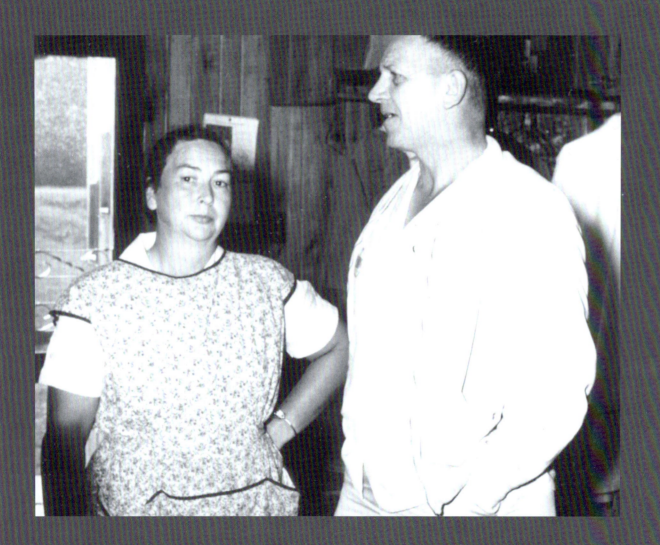

CAMP ROY-EL

Over the years, Hickory has hosted more than downhill and cross-country skiers. Hikers, runners, day campers and disc golfers are just some of the groups who have enjoyed Hickory's hills. While these popular uses are well known, a lesser-known fledgling operation with broad impact — Camp Roy-El — began at Hickory in the early 1950s when the polio epidemic devastated the lives of hundreds of children.

Physical therapist Roy Brigman spent his career at Traverse City's Munson Hospital, helping physically handicapped children and young polio victims become more mobile. Brigman and his wife, Ellen, both strong believers in outdoor recreation for children, made it their mission to provide his patients with a universal childhood tradition: summer camp.

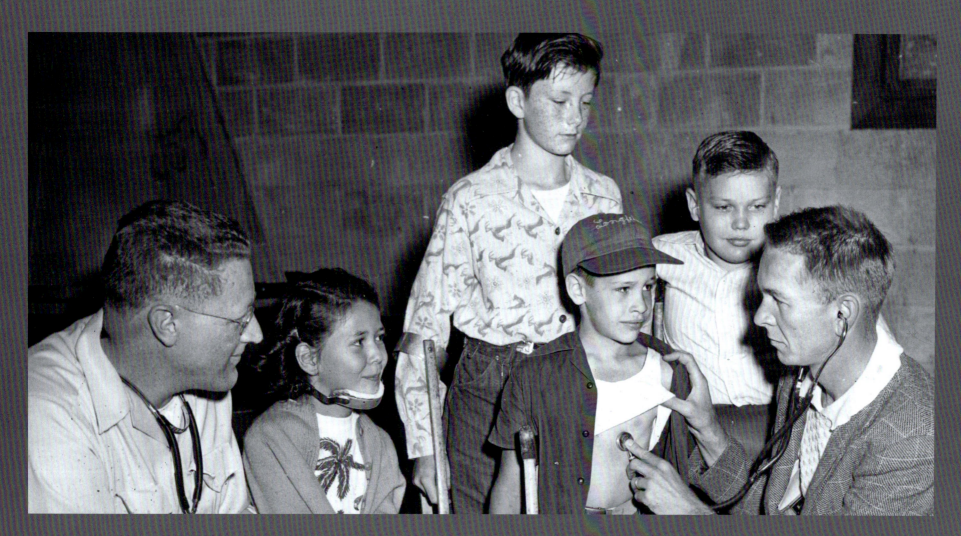

38   one: Humble Hill, Big Vision

In August 1952, the Brigmans began a summer camp for disabled youth. The location: Hickory Hills, a woodsy, safe destination that could be used without charge. The couple borrowed tents, cots and other camping equipment from the Girl Scouts and solicited donations from the local March of Dimes and Easter Seals societies to purchase more supplies.

The camp's first fifteen "handicampers," as they were fondly called, ranged in age from eight to sixteen. Local volunteers and Girl Scout "teenaiders" camped alongside the handicampers to provide care and assistance. Camp activities included daily flag raising, fishing in Grand Traverse Bay, cooking over open fires and archery at the base of Pete. Two local physicians gave free physical examinations to the campers in Hickory's lodge.

Named by campers in honor of Roy and Ellen, Camp Roy-El became the only free summer camping destination for area handicapped children — with the important benefit of providing their parents a much-appreciated weeklong vacation.

A huge success for campers, families and the Brigmans alike, Camp Roy-El returned to Hickory the summer of 1953 with twenty campers, including twelve veteran campers from the summer before. Hickory proved an ideal campground in many ways, but it couldn't offer swimming — an important summer camp activity. So, the following summer, the Brigmans said good-bye to Hickory and packed up and moved camp to Traverse City's Twin Lakes site. For the next thirty-seven summers, Camp Roy-El became a destination for more than eight hundred handicapped youth campers. Camp Roy-El closed permanently in 1991, after several other specialized camps had opened throughout Michigan. Many had finally recognized what the Brigmans had known decades ago — disabled youth need and benefit from outdoor recreation.

Camp Roy-El remains a proud moment in Hickory's history. Like Hickory, Camp Roy-El invited children, deserving yet unserved, to enjoy recreation at no cost. The camp was born in a time when volunteers such as the Brigmans and Hickory's founders embraced "can-do" attitudes, forging ahead and believing great things would result. The Brigmans' daughter, Kathy (Brigman) Woods, sums it up well: "Hickory gave us a great start. It was because Camp Roy-El was successful there that we were able to grow. Hickory did so much for us."

one: Humble Hill, Big Vision 41

two

EMERGING SPORT, LEGENDARY LEADER

A BORN LEADER

Hans "Peppi" Teichner didn't grow up easily, but he grew up tough. Despite having been born with a clubfoot and having developed asthma some years later, he played in the mountains like other children in his native Germany — learning to hike, climb and even ski. But Teichner had a competitive edge and drive that made him stand out. A graduate of the University of Munich, he became an outstanding skier, tennis player and national track star. In 1928, as a young but exceptional skier, Teichner raced for Germany's national ski team.

In preparation for the 1936 Olympics, Spain's Olympic ski team sought the natural leader for its coach. So, in 1933, Teichner took the opportunity not only to further his skiing career but also to leave the unrest of Nazi Germany for Spain. What started out as a promising Olympic coaching career, however, ended with Teichner leading a smuggling ring for government loyalists when the Spanish Civil War erupted. Although the twenty-eight-year-old appeared to be instructing classes of innocent ski enthusiasts, Teichner actually provided escape for those fleeing Spain's new fascist regime. Under his lead, groups skied across the Pyrenees to freedom in France. "He pretended to be leading a ski class and then skied back alone for the next group," says Teichner's daughter, Martha Teichner. When he was finally discovered by Franco's forces (which included members of the Spanish Olympic team he coached), Teichner "had a price put on his head."

Peppi was a major factor...a new light shining in the community.

Helen Milliken

two: Emerging Sport, Legendary Leader 45

BECOMING AMERICAN: THE 10TH MOUNTAIN DIVISION

Forced to flee Spain, Teichner emigrated to the United States on Armistice Day 1937. Following work as a ranch hand in Wyoming, Teichner returned to his real love, alpine ski instruction at the popular Sun Valley Resort in Idaho. He taught and skied there until the onset of the United States' involvement in World War II.

Although a recent immigrant himself, Teichner volunteered for military service and was assigned to the 10th Mountain Division, a highly specialized Army combat division. Specifically trained for winter warfare in the mountains of Europe, the men of the 10th Mountain Division were tough. Knowing how to ski and survive in the mountains was just one of the specialized skills — by then second nature to Teichner — that were required of these men. The military branch teamed up with the National Ski Patrol in this unique partnership to recruit thousands of volunteer skiers for both training and combat with the newly formed unit. Teichner taught many of these men to ski and rock climb. The division's heroic actions in the Italian Alps in 1945 set the stage for the German Army's surrender in Italy.

After his service with the 10th Mountain Division, Teichner entered officer candidate school and was commissioned a second lieutenant. Fluent in five languages, Teichner served the Army with military intelligence by speaking with prisoners of war.

TALENT TRAVELS TO TRAVERSE CITY

Following the war, Teichner and other 10th Mountain Division men did what they knew best. They applied their talents to what was still a fledgling ski industry, relocating to resort towns throughout the country. Teichner moved to Aspen.

In 1946, Art Huey, then head of the area's Leelanau School, was heavily involved in the early development of a local ski resort called Sugar Loaf. Huey personally recruited Teichner to assist with the resort's trail design and instruction program. While popular in America's West, skiing had not yet taken hold in the Midwest or in Michigan. Tentative at first, Teichner initially commuted between Aspen and his new job in northern Michigan. Although he never intended to stay in Michigan, Teichner ultimately decided "there was fertile ground in northern Michigan to interest people in skiing," remembers his daughter, Martha. Little did Teichner know the impact his contribution to skiing would have on the Traverse City region, including his role with Ci-Bo, Hickory and, later, Holiday Hills.

Teichner proved instrumental in Sugar Loaf's early success, which included hosting the Midwest's best racers at the United States Ski Association's (USSA) Central Division downhill and slalom championships. The small resort received national media attention in those years, much due to Teichner's involvement.

His passion for skiing could not be contained; it went beyond the hills of Sugar Loaf. He worked with the City of Traverse City in the development of both Ci-Bo and Hickory Hills. "My father was like the circus master when skiing came to town," remembers Martha. "He was a super-salesman for skiing. He had this tremendously charismatic personality and had a huge following of adults and children who adored him. He had the perfect combination of teacher and showman." Both attributes were critical to Hickory's success in those early years.

A PUBLIC SCHOOL SKI SCHOOL

While Teichner deserves recognition for his role as a promoter of community skiing in Traverse City, ski instruction remains his greatest single contribution. With his thick German accent, Teichner could be heard throughout the day booming, "Ben zhee knees! Ben zhee knees!" Barbara Sherberneau recalls the good-natured head instructor shaking his head while teaching the snowplow and saying, "I said put tips together and push out with the heels. I did NOT say cross the skis."

Teichner seemed to possess natural teaching abilities. Whether these talents were attributable to his early physical struggles or his innate leadership skills, Teichner "could get people to achieve something that they did not believe they could achieve." Martha explains her father's strong belief in athletic opportunities for children: "If you can develop your skills as an athlete and the values that go along with competition, it will set you up for a successful life."

An expert technician and instructor, Teichner also possessed a clear vision of how instruction should be provided for area youth. Martha recalls her father's dream for "a public school–type system for skiing, where if you wanted to ski, there would be a way to do it, even if you could not afford it." Teichner and Hickory's founders were entirely consistent in their combined vision: skiing and instruction must be provided for all who want them, not just those who can afford them. Their concept of affordable skiing in the Traverse area stuck.

A LEADER OF ATHLETES

As a constant advocate for the sport, Teichner successfully lobbied the Michigan High School Athletic Association (MHSAA) to endorse skiing as an interscholastic sport in 1953. Trusted by the ski community, he served as chief of race for the very first high school Lower Peninsula Regionals, the only state championship meet at that time, held at Sugar Loaf in 1954. His Hickory racers, Barbara Sherberneau and Larry Bensley, raced their way to championships there. Teichner continued to serve the fledgling ski industry and in 1956 volunteered on the race committee for the Lower Peninsula Championship meet hosted by the Grand Traverse Ski Club at Hickory Hills.

Teichner taught on and off the slopes with authority. As a teacher at The Leelanau School, he still found time to coach. Teichner possessed endless energy for the sport of ski racing and even accompanied northern Michigan racers to Central Division and USSA races. Teichner opened doors for northern Michigan youth, traveling with them to Aspen so they could experience real mountains. Pete Rennie recalls an Aspen trip hosted by Teichner: "It was the first time I saw him let loose and really ski. We were all amazed. We couldn't even keep up. He was a beautiful skier." Rennie remembers Teichner not only as a artful skier but also as "an amazing person. We all learned a lot from him."

In 1957, at the young age of forty-nine, Teichner died, leaving behind his wife, Miriam, and nine-year-old daughter, Martha. Despite a short life and even shorter stay in northern Michigan, Teichner left a long legacy. He brought a passion for the sport of ski racing to the area. As an Olympic coach and 10th Mountain Division instructor, he not only imparted expert technical instruction to young skiers but did so with a gentle but firm authority. Teichner relentlessly advocated for competitive opportunities and the development of local ski areas. Ultimately, his vision of public school ski instruction laid the foundation for strong local support and a lasting commitment to welcome all young athletes to the sport.

Peppi Teichner, known as Michigan's "Father of Skiing," was inducted into the U.S. Ski Hall of Fame in 1967.

three

SMALL TOWN, BIG WORLD

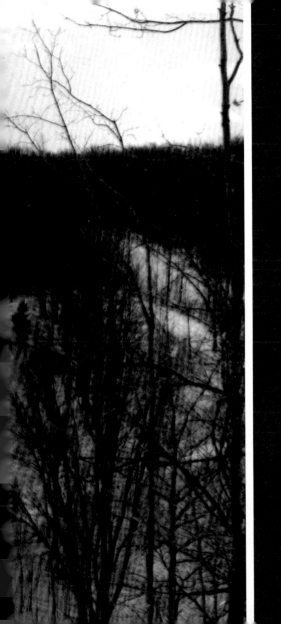

A SMALL TOWN EMBRACES A NEW SPORT

Only a few alpine ski areas existed in Michigan before World War II, including Hanson Hills in Grayling, the Otsego Club in Gaylord and Caberfae Peaks in Cadillac.

After the war, the return of the 10th Mountain Division generated greater attention to and interest in the sport of downhill skiing. The celebrity dynamic, combined with a robust postwar economy, fueled ski fever across the United States and into the Midwest. Michigan's existing ski industry soon had company. In the late 1940s, Everett Kircher built Boyne Mountain, and Art Huey, along with local investors, launched the development of Leelanau County's Sugar Loaf Winter Sports Area.

Until that time, Traverse City had remained dormant in the winter. Most residents hibernated from November through March. As Oscar (Swede) Johnson's son, Clayton Johnson, recalls, "The only thing to do was shovel." But when Traverse City's Ci-Bo opened in 1950, and Hickory Hills in 1952, thousands of children began to ski — most of them for free. With the bright lights of Hickory calling, long winter nights spent hibernating became a thing of the past.

Hickory is the seed; it's where it all begins.

Chris MacInnes

LEARNING THE ROPES

Peppi Teichner understood that new skiers need knowledge of the basics and strong technique. His philosophy that ski instruction should follow a public school model — open to all — underscored the value of volunteerism and outside financial support for ski instruction programs. For decades, volunteer instructors and local businesses and organizations provided free instruction at Hickory Hills.

THE RECORD-EAGLE SKI SCHOOL

As the first of many free instruction programs, Traverse City's Record-Eagle Ski School at Ci-Bo set the tone. Ski School Director Teichner needed help. He scouted for those who already knew how to ski. Volunteer recruits, adults and students alike, participated in an instructors' course. They completed the short course and immediately began to teach. "The children were fearless and easy to teach," recalls volunteer instructor Helen Milliken.

At Hickory, the Record-Eagle Ski School continued to rely on young volunteer talent. "Ben Taylor decided that we ought to be teaching instead of terrorizing the slopes, so he made a couple of us ski instructors in the Record-Eagle Ski School," Fitch Williams recalls. "There I was, a little kid, with a class full of twenty- and thirty-year-olds, teaching them stem christies. I'd ski backwards to tell them what they were doing wrong. After they found out I could ski backwards better than they could ski forward, they listened to everything I said. By the time we were finished, they were following me down the hill. Ben was very clever."

Graduates of the ski school received a highly coveted patch. Len Ligon, one of Traverse City's most medaled racers, still remembers his Record-Eagle Ski School patch: "I was really, really proud of that patch." Starting with just one hundred eager students at Ci-Bo, the Record-Eagle Ski School has since graduated more than thirty thousand skiers.

"Hickory Hills was the cradle of skiing in the Grand Traverse area and birthed a huge interest in a new sport via the *Record-Eagle* free skiing lessons and racing program," attests Marshall Carr, who learned to ski under Hickory's lights. "It was a key factor in what would become a standard recreational activity for families. I still ski blues and blacks in my seventy-first year, and I still think I'm a racer when I do. It all goes back to Hickory Hills."

The Record-Eagle Ski School allowed us to be proficient enough to truly enjoy skiing.

Dick Swan

The Record-Eagle Ski School was the beginning. It was free – a gift to literally thousands of kids.

Susan Elliott McGarry

60 three: Small Town, Big World

SKI LIKE STEIN

Few international skiers become local names. Stein Eriksen, however, Norway's top alpine racer, a 1952 Winter Olympic medalist and the first-ever World Champion triple gold medalist in 1954, ventured to northern Michigan to bring world-class ski technique to the Midwest.

Personally recruited by Everett Kircher, the visionary developer of Boyne Mountain, Eriksen left Norway at the age of twenty-six to take the position as Boyne Mountain's ski school director. And just as Kircher intended, Eriksen's good looks and athleticism quickly dazzled Michigan skiers. Aware of his celebrity status, Eriksen not only developed Boyne's ski school into a popular and successful program but also promoted himself. He even advertised his personal technique, in particular his "reverse-shoulder," with the motto "Ski Like Stein." He performed weekly shows at Boyne Mountain showcasing his style and technique. Eriksen and Boyne were an instant hit. The camera loved him, as did everyone else. In part due to Eriksen's appeal, Boyne became the hot ski destination for Midwest skiers.

Hickory wanted in on the Eriksen action. In 1955, members of the Kiwanis Club of Traverse City asked Kircher whether Boyne would loan Eriksen to Hickory's program, specifically to the ski school sponsored by the Kiwanis Club. With Kircher's blessing, Eriksen commuted twice each week to Hickory, providing pizzazz to Hickory's budding program. An added benefit: Eriksen brought with him several visiting northern European instructors, then residents at Boyne. With white turtlenecks, Norwegian sweaters and sleek race jackets embroidered with Boyne Mountain's insignia, the instructors cut a smooth path.

three: Small Town, Big World

three: Small Town, Big World

Helen Milliken remembers Eriksen's style: "He was a fashionista. He wore beautiful sweaters and sometimes changed twice a day."

Francie Dorman recalls the popularity of those sweaters and how young skiers idolized Eriksen: "Mickey Joynt and the Rennie boys wore sweaters like Stein Eriksen. Mickey's mother knitted ones just like Stein's."

Eriksen amazed young Hickory racers — and their parents — with his talent. "Stein was the most beautiful skier I've ever seen in my life. We all tried to ski like him," recalls Pete Rennie. Eriksen brought more than just style and technique to Hickory; in many ways, he added a bigger worldview. Dick Swan, only thirteen when he skied under Eriksen, credits him with the suggestion that the Hickory Hills Ski Club change its name to the Grand Traverse Ski Club. Eriksen encouraged the change, stating, "Wherever your racers are, the world will know where they came from." The champion was right. Skiers everywhere know Grand Traverse Ski Club racers — and that they hail from Hickory.

After just two years, Eriksen left the small but mighty hills of Michigan for bigger resorts, including Heavenly Valley, Aspen Highlands, Snowmass and Sugarbush. He retired as director of skiing at Deer Valley, leaving a lodge there that bears his name. Eriksen's impact on small-town northern Michigan has not been forgotten. Dorman smiles at the memory: "Our boys still cherish and even wear those Norwegian sweaters that survived all these years. In fact they swipe them from each other when the opportunity arises."

THE KIWANIS SKI SCHOOL

Beginning skiers who earned the Record-Eagle Ski School patch wanted more instruction. Loren Bensley, Hickory founder and member of the Kiwanis Club of Traverse City, approached his fellow Kiwanians for sponsorship of a new ski school. The Kiwanis Ski School began in 1953, offering intermediate ski instruction. Similar to the Record-Eagle school, it utilized many of the same volunteer instructors and awarded a Kiwanis Ski School patch upon completion. That patch, too, became a badge of pride.

The Kiwanis Ski School soon bolstered its credentials. In 1955, Hickory leaders convinced Boyne Mountain's Kircher to loan Hickory more experienced instructors. At the time, Royce Asher, a former Sun Valley ski instructor and coach for the U.S. Army Ski Team in Europe, served as assistant director for Stein Eriksen's ski school at Boyne. First on loan to Hickory, Asher quickly became a full-time Hickory instructor. He relocated to Traverse City, taking the position of head ski professional at Hickory. Responsible for the Kiwanis program, Asher used his connections to encourage other Boyne instructors to teach at Hickory's Kiwanis Ski School. Hickory's advanced skiers were given the unusual opportunity to learn from the best.

"One year, Stein Eriksen, the Norwegian [Olympic] gold medal winner, gave us lessons showing us his reverse-shoulder technique. We even watched him doing his aerial tricks on Old Pete," remembers Meredith Raftshol Amon. "What a gift they gave to the youth of Traverse City. I will be forever grateful for the wonderful opportunity to ski."

THE MILLIKEN SKI SCHOOL

Teichner's influence went beyond the ski hill. He had a working relationship with the Milliken family and so approached them to sponsor a third ski school at Hickory. And by utilizing volunteer instructors, the Milliken Ski School provided night instruction under the lights at Hickory from the mid-1950s into the 1960s.

TEAM AUSTRIA

Hickory benefited from its relationship with Boyne Mountain through the years, especially Hickory's ski schools and instructors. In the late 1960s, Boyne Mountain became host to several Austrian instructors, former Olympians and Austrian National Team members who began to revolutionize ski racing technique in northern Michigan. Impressed by the instructors' style and technique, Grand Traverse Ski Club board member Ted Kramer Sr. asked Kircher to allow Boyne's Austrian instructors to train with Hickory's ski club racers a few nights during the week. With Kircher's approval, the Austrians, eager for additional income, agreed to coach the race clinics.

These expert race instructors wearing Boyne parkas impressed Hickory racers. "Attendance was usually great when the Austrians were teaching. The girls were often swooning over their European instructors," recalls racer Tammy Hagerty.

Bob Core describes how there were "Hugos, Esis and Rainers everywhere — such a talented group of former Olympians and Austrian National Ski Team members coaching Hickory kids."

Nick Nixon remembers the Austrian coaches as "tall and fit with marvelous accents. They were really cool."

Ted Kramer Jr. understood the impact of his father's proposal: "We didn't have any formal race instruction before that. They taught us real technique."

Through quality instruction programs, supportive partnerships and innovative efforts to bring in outside talent, Hickory and the ski club began to earn their reputations for producing some of the toughest racers in Michigan. "I was surprised by them," says Austrian Coach Robert Kirschlager. "Some of them showed tremendous talent. From the little hills of northern Michigan come some of the best skiers."

The best thing about Hickory is the exposure, the opportunity to expose young people to skiing. The runs are short; you have to utilize what you've got.

Robert Kirschlager

SMALL PATCHES, GREAT FUN

When Hickory opened in 1952, a season ski pass — free to city residents — was a simple embroidered patch. Resident skiers picked up a newly issued patch at the beginning of each season at city hall. Excited about the new season's color, they sewed the patch to the arm of their parkas.

In 1958, the city began to charge a small fee for the season patch in an effort to offset operational costs at Hickory — fifty cents for children and one dollar for adults. Despite modestly increased fees over the years, the city and Hickory have remained true to the original mission: to provide affordable skiing for all. Jan Elliott Shugart sums up the Hickory experience: "It was a fair, equitable playground for all. Every kid got a chance to ski; every kid could compete in the ski club; every kid could get a ride home with someone. Thank you to the City of Traverse City for the foresight to have a municipal ski area for all."

How do you put a price on youth recreation?

Lauren Vaughn, Traverse City Parks and Recreation Superintendent

How many youth can say that they have a ski area in their neighborhood where they can ski after school, go home for dinner and ski again under the lights in the evening with no charge?

Meredith Raftshol Amon

> My parents took me to Trude Hardware on Front Street for my first skis, hickory skis with bear trap bindings.
>
> Jack Keyes

GEARING UP

Skiers needed gear to take advantage of the emerging sport. In 1950, local hardware stores and the Army surplus store responded to the mounting excitement by stocking ski equipment. Inventory sold out too fast to restock, as dozens of kids added skis, boots and bindings to their Christmas wish lists. The skis were twenty dollars, boots fifteen and bindings five, but the new skill and lifelong passion the young skiers were about to gain were invaluable.

As the ski industry boomed, equipment became more specialized, and specialty sports stores began popping up throughout Traverse City. A new ski culture, complete with the ski shop, took hold.

Peppi Teichner and his wife, Miriam, operated one of Traverse City's first ski shops, Peppi's Corner, located in the basement of Milliken's Department Store. The shop drew many enthusiasts with its "very fine European imported ski apparel and equipment." Peppi's daughter, Martha, recalls skiers flocking to the shop in the early winter season, including the developer of Crystal Mountain, George Petritz, who outfitted his entire family there for the ski season.

Specialty stores also brought variety. Tom Joynt, the first executive director for the Central Division of the United States Ski Association (headquartered in downtown Traverse City), owned Bilmar sports shop and offered package deals for skis, boots and poles.

Don Orr began selling skis in the 1950s out of the Evans Paint store before he opened his own ski store. In 1959, Orr and a few buddies built the distinctive chalet-styled Don Orr Ski Haus.

Over the decades, increased demand and healthy competition led to additional stores selling specialty ski equipment in Traverse City, including Hamilton's, Matterhorn, Wilhelm's, Boyne Country Sports and Brick Wheels, to name a few.

Equipment design and style evolved rapidly with the sport. Long, stiff hickory skis gave way to newer models. In the late 1950s, metal skis were introduced. Head skis, carried by both Orr and Bilmars, proved especially successful for area skiers. Head skis enjoyed a strong local following, and Howard Head often visited northern Michigan to scout young talent willing

to experiment with his new skis. "He talked with us and sent us home with several pairs of experimental skis. We then tried and returned them with an evaluation of their performance," recalls Marshall Carr. "For twenty-five dollars, you could send your Head skis back to the factory every summer, and they would rebuild the whole bottom with a new base and very sharp edges, and they looked like new. It was a great deal!"

By the early 1960s, local shops replaced leather-strapped bindings with release-toe bindings under a variety of brand names, including A&T, Cubco and Marker. A clever local physician with an entrepreneurial spirit, Dr. Phil Wiley, invented his own ski binding called the Wiley-omatic. Promoted throughout the Midwest, the binding was picked up by shops, and Wiley's son, Paul, raced every high school race on the bindings his father developed.

three: Small Town, Big World

SMALL BUDGET, BOLD ENTHUSIASM

For thirty-three years, Vojin Baic brought enthusiasm and fresh ideas to his job as Traverse City's director of Parks and Recreation. A man with a "can-do" attitude, Baic was a perfect fit to manage not only the city's recreation department but also its biggest park, Hickory Hills.

Born in 1929, Baic grew up in Belgrade, Yugoslavia. During the Nazi occupation, his father was imprisoned and one of his sisters sent to a concentration camp in Germany. While trying to cope in Eastern Europe's postwar communist regime, Baic was expelled from school due to his "anticommunist youth activities."

A fierce athlete, Baic cross-country skied and rowed for the Yugoslavian National and Olympic teams. In 1949, while in Amsterdam for the World Rowing Championships, he defected, later emigrating to the United States. After service in the Korean War, he attended Marquette University, where he continued to cross-country ski. Baic became the U.S. Cross Country Ski Chairman and coached from 1959 to 1966.

In 1966, Baic moved to Traverse City as the Central Division of the United States Ski Association (CUSSA) national competition manager. When CUSSA's offices were relocated to

Here is a man who came from behind the Iron Curtain and can and does teach us, each and every one of us, the values of freedom and active citizenship. There is no person in this area that has done as much for the young people.

Les Biederman

Chicago, Baic knew what job he wanted in Traverse City: Parks and Recreation director. The city had no such position, however, so Baic approached the city manager and convinced him to try Baic out for six months. He offered to do the job for free: "Then," Baic said, "you can pay me what I'm worth." Baic soon had the new job and a salary.

Through his boundless and infectious energy, Baic established citywide instruction, camps and competition for cross-country skiing, touch football, tennis and swimming. He developed areawide cross-country ski trails, bike trails, physical fitness and training programs and expanded recreational events for the National Cherry Festival. He developed the area's first cross-country skiing program and also coached many of Hickory's alpine racers.

Baic befriended Traverse City residents of all ages and from all walks of life. As a young John Robert Williams said, "He has rubbed a little competitive spirit into all that come in contact with him. He gets involved with everything of interest in the community, puts his sparky touch to it and BOOM! This man is hyperactive in the community. Not a day goes by that he isn't rubbing shoulders with everyone at city hall, his neighbors, his family and his sporting companions."

Baic believed that city recreation programs should be free of charge. He solicited friends and local businesses — anyone who had something to offer. "When we needed money, it was there," recalls Baic. He even convinced Dick Mattern of Matterhorn Sports to offer free rentals at Hickory and as a result almost lost his job.

In 1973, the Traverse Area Chamber of Commerce honored Baic with its Distinguished Citizen Award. According to a group of young people who had written in support of Baic's nomination for the award, "[Baic was] concerned for people and always trying to make things as economical as possible so that the financial role [would] not become a barrier for the participants." The youth who benefited from Baic's generosity said as much: "His enthusiasm rubbed off on many people. He would remind us that people on earth are here only for one reason — 'to help each other.'"

And Baic did help people. Clark Phelps Sr. said, "He stimulated many to levels of accomplishment they would never have reached on their own."

Baic served as the city's recreation director until he retired in 1991. His contributions to area recreation, especially for youth, remain unmatched. Hickory Hills in particular benefited from Baic's goodwill, generous works and dedication. And true to his philosophy that recreation should be free, Baic to this day believes "the main priority of Hickory should be affordability."

four

PINT-SIZED CLUB, HUGE IMPROVEMENTS

By 1952, novice skiers became experts at navigating Hickory's terrain. Eager for more racing opportunity, many yearned to race for the United States Ski Association (USSA). USSA, however, required racers to have a ski club affiliation. Hickory soon became home to the Hickory Hills Ski Club. Early on, Hickory racers represented the ski club at races held throughout the Midwest, accompanied by Coaches Peppi Teichner, Don Orr and Jack Bensley. In 1955, Hickory's race instruction program merged with the race program offered at Holiday Hills, and the club became the Grand Traverse Ski Club. Through promotion of the sport, quality instruction and healthy competition, the Grand Traverse Ski Club nurtured Hickory with innovation, manpower and volunteerism, combined with a passion for racing.

SAFETY FIRST

John Hunter Merrill — or "Jack" to most — started Hickory's first ski patrol. Instrumental in the development of Hickory, he served on Hickory's first board of directors. As Hickory's manager and a pioneer member of the Grand Traverse Ski Club, Merrill focused on safety and instruction at a time when injuries were all too common because of long, inflexible skis and old-style bindings.

With John Norton's assistance, Merrill began recruiting young proficient skiers for the ski patrol. One such early recruit, Pete Rennie, just twelve when asked to join, felt honored to be chosen. "The first time I put on that ski patrol parka — that was the greatest thing," recalls Rennie.

"He really helped get the ski patrol going. He was all about teaching children how to ski," says granddaughter Allison Merrill.

Merrill passed away in 1959 at the young age of thirty-seven before accomplishing his goals for Hickory's budding ski patrol. Merrill's loss was felt throughout the small

Jack Merrill wore a rust-colored light parka over a sweater so the wind billowed around his chest as he flew down the hill.

Lisa Oddy-Grace

four: Pint-sized Club, Huge Improvements

Hickory community. In his honor, Jack Bensley organized several fundraisers to continue what Merrill had started. Ski club and community members helped fund a new ski patrol room at Hickory, a project Merrill had been working on before his death. "Jack was loved by everyone in the community," recalls Allison Merrill. "That's all my relatives ever talked about, how much they loved Jack."

When Merrill's son, Jim, died in the early 1990s, Merrill family friend and Hickory Coach Sandy Blumenfeld organized the Merrill Memorial Race, described by Blumenfeld as one way "to honor the entire Merrill family for their contribution to Traverse City skiing and ski racing." Held at Hickory for many years, the Merrill Memorial Race sported high school skiers, little racers and even old-timers.

"Those who raced to remember also remembered to race," recalls Dave Merrill of the event honoring his brother and father.

A plaque dedicated to Merrill — the man who started it all — still hangs in Hickory's Merrill Ski Patrol Room.

The safety record of Hickory Hills is phenomenal, far above the national average, and I like to think it's due in part to a farsighted program of instruction the moment the youngsters get their skis.

John Norton, *Mid-West Skier*, January 15, 1955

four: Pint-sized Club, Huge Improvements

RACER READY?

Sunday races at Hickory are the backbone of the ski club's race program and a rallying point for the volunteer commitment that contributes to Hickory's staying power. Sunday races continue to bring everyone together for one goal: healthy competition and speed. With racer age groups starting at ages zero to eight and topping out at sixteen and over, skiers of every size and shape race.

In 1952, and for decades after, the uniforms, race provisions and race and timing equipment were all handcrafted. The ski club remained current, and equipment was updated as often as possible. Primitive by modern standards, the equipment changed through creativity and innovation. Gatekeepers wore hand-sewn black and gold bibs — clearly visible to racers. Ski club moms sewed numbered bibs for every racer.

Dale Wares, ski club president in 1959 and 1960, supervised the design, development and construction of bamboo painted gates and state-of-the-art timing equipment. The timer was built with its own mobile transport — a rustic homemade toboggan. Equipment designed by club members, out of necessity and a spirit of improvement, became a model followed by other ski organizations throughout the country.

In the late 1960s, Bob Core, an electrical engineer, and Dick Babel, a telephone company employee, wired the hills for timing and audio equipment, installing timing gear via portable radios. Mary Hazelton remembers, "Results were calculated to the tenth of a second using a hand-cranked adding machine." Surprisingly, she insists "there were very few ties."

Despite the ski club's "high-tech" timing equipment, Joe Elliott recalls, "starting the races with a flagger at the bottom of the hill, then switching to radio, required a watchful eye of the starter as to whether you jumped the gun. It made for some interesting starts."

four: Pint-sized Club, Huge Improvements

For many years, the ski club hosted the area's high school regional meet at Hickory. Not only was the race equipment far superior to that of other clubs, but also the dedication of the club's hardworking volunteers made Hickory an ideal destination. "We had a parent for each gate," Gil Bogley remembers.

So many parents volunteered that, according to Lorna Ameel, "it was the ones who didn't work who stood out."

Carl Madion also notes that it wasn't just parents of skiers who volunteered: "There were certain people who were not even parents, but they were devoted to skiing and the ski club. They'd be there every single Sunday morning, ready to help."

We wore our ski clothes to church so we could make it to Sunday races on time.

Meg Wilson Godfrey

I started skiing before I was actually tall enough to reach the tow ropes, so I rode up between one of my brother's legs.

Julie Lane Leep

TROPHIES ARE FOR SUCKERS

In addition to the thrill of victory, colored ribbons and end-of-season trophies have drawn Grand Traverse Ski Club racers to Hickory's Sunday races since 1952. Awards didn't include just hardware, however.

The most coveted treats for Sunday racers in the 1960s were the large cellophane-wrapped sweet-n-sour lollipops that came in an assortment of mouthwatering flavors. A long-standing tradition at Sunday races for many years, the suckers were handed out even to the youngest racers simply for completing the race.

Inspired by a ski school in New Hampshire run by Olympic skier Andrea Mead Lawrence, Anne Bogley started the Grand Traverse Ski Club's lollipop awards with help from other ski club moms. One of Meg Wilson Godfrey's fondest memories remains "the lollipop I received even after missing every single gate."

RACE CLINICS

Undoubtedly, through its instruction programs and Sunday races, Hickory produced excellent racers. But the ski club recognized that some gaps existed and in 1976 determined that a comprehensive instruction program was necessary. Sanford Blumenfeld and Jerry Stanek approached Paul Ameel, then ski club president, with a proposal specifically designed for a broader youth population — from the youngest skiers through high school–age students. Their proposal, modeled after Coach Jim Ooley's (Traverse City's well-respected varsity football coach) football program, focused on using former ski club racers as coaches. The key: involve children in what would become a feeder program, progressing through structured, continuous instruction until they enter high school. With enthusiastic support for Blumenfeld and Stanek's proposal, the ski club began offering "learn to ski" classes and race clinics for all ages several times each week.

BRIDGING THE GAP

Due to the expense of the sport and a growing interest in freestyle skiing and snowboarding in the 1990s, the number of downhill racers at the high school level declined. Unwilling to accept the trend, Grand Traverse Ski Club President Matt Madion and his wife, Jody, attempted to reverse it. The couple helped develop a formal middle school instruction program and race team. Working with local middle schools, the ski club organized the team, hired coaches and found race venues. With the new interscholastic program, teen racers returned to Hickory, their numbers growing from a mere half dozen in the program's first year to nearly fifty racers in later years.

With a formal middle school program in place, the ski club's continuum of instruction at Hickory became complete. Traverse City's high school teams remained formidable. Former high school varsity Coach Jerry Stanek once observed that "the middle school team was the best program the ski club created. It saved our high school teams."

Fiercely committed to quality ski instruction and junior race programs, the Grand Traverse Ski Club produced powerhouse racers who advanced from Sunday races to varsity high school and collegiate teams — and even to World Cup circuits.

THE MIDWEST'S LARGEST SKI SWAP

By November, winter is in the air. Traverse City skiers young and old begin the frenzy of pulling gear from summer storage, taking inventory, marking the calendar and setting clocks for 5:00 a.m. wake-up calls. It's ski sale time. The goal: be in line for first-dibs viewing, wheeling and dealing and buying and selling gear.

Inspired by the Saginaw Ski Club, Grand Traverse Ski Club parent and volunteer Claire Nixon organized the club's first annual used-equipment sale in 1961. Originally dubbed the "rummage sale" and held at Waple's in downtown Traverse City's Chrysler dealership storefront, the sale had "such a little bit of equipment it was hysterical," recalls ski club mom Lorna Ameel.

Over the years, the sale has only grown bigger. According to Nixon, "It started slow but became successful. We never gave up. People really looked forward to it." Venues have changed to accommodate the sheer volume of inventory and have included the Traverse City Yacht Club, Max's Service, Glenn Loomis Elementary School, the Park Place Dome and Traverse City Central High School. The sale, billed as "the Midwest's largest ski swap," has finally settled in at Traverse City's Junior High School, now called Traverse City West Middle School.

With winter and skiing in the air, an infectious buzz in the gymnasium fuels the spirit of volunteerism every year. The

Grand Traverse Ski Club recruits hundreds of volunteers, young and old alike, for the three-day extravaganza. They make it all happen: setup, equipment check-in, inventory, labeling, ticket distribution, sales, professional equipment advice and fitting, checkout, accounting and, finally, teardown and cleanup. It is a monumental task, but fifty years of practice make an almost perfect operation.

Skiers drop off gently used equipment at the Friday evening check-in, and volunteers assist with pricing. Families flock to the Saturday sale to suit their young skiers with affordable equipment. Late Sunday afternoon, sellers return to collect sales proceeds.

While equipment supply and demand and the sport's popularity have changed over time, the ski sale has grown to be a huge success. In the 1970s, demand for merchandise was so high that the club hired local police as overnight security. In recent years, die-hards have even camped out overnight to ensure early access to highly coveted items.

Part fundraiser, part community service, the event boasts sales of more than $1 million from 2000 to 2010. The proceeds — twenty percent of every sale goes to the ski club — have funded significant improvements at Hickory. Michael "Mac" McClelland, who has held the unenviable position of ski sale chair since 2009, says, "The ski sale is really a starting point — getting great equipment at an affordable price, raising money for the ski club's instructional programs and an opportunity for everyone to get together and kick off winter." The ski sale, like the club's other activities, upholds the club's mission and that of its home, Hickory: ensuring affordable access to skiing for youth.

PARTNERSHIP MEANS IMPROVEMENTS

Hickory Hills, one of the few remaining public ski parks in the country, would not exist without the ongoing support of the City of Traverse City. Dedicated to safe, affordable recreational opportunities for area youth, the city has continued to recognize the importance of its original vision.

In this endeavor, the city has had many generous public and private partners. Throughout Hickory's development, the park's biggest supporter has been the Grand Traverse Ski Club and its tireless volunteers.

This municipal/nonprofit partnership fueled Hickory's early programmatic success and provided for subsequent capital improvements. The club's first fundraiser for Hickory, a benefit dinner hosted by Pete Batsakis in 1952, began a philanthropic tradition. Through the generosity of community members and local charities, the Grand Traverse Ski Club has raised more than $300,000 for Hickory's capital improvements and equipment upgrades. The ski club's programs and dedicated volunteers, along with the city's support, have allowed youth to ski and race in top-notch instructional programs at affordable prices.

Skiing at Hickory Hills is free to residents of the city. Anyone joining the Club will have the satisfaction of knowing that his money will be used to improve slopes, provide new lighting, and promote better skiing in the Hickory Hills area.

Don Orr, Hickory Hills Ski Club's first president

IMPROVEMENTS

1965: The ski club, realizing it needed an equipment storage shed, mailed a simple flier seeking donations and manual labor: carpenters, electricians, painters and even "lousy carpenters that can hand stuff to somebody." The ski club built the shed in just a few days.

1973: In an effort to expand Hickory's skiable slopes and maintain excellent racing conditions, the ski club purchased Hickory's first automated snow groomer and packer — manual grooming became a thing of the past. Skiers no longer had to "sidestep for hours, trying to get everything packed down," as Pete Rennie remembers he and his friends often did in the 1950s. Hickory employees "wouldn't turn the tow ropes on until the hills were packed down, so it was up to the day skiers to do it." With the new groomer, the natural moguls on Pete, either dreaded or loved, became a memory of the past.

1984: Aiming to make Pete more accessible and user-friendly, the ski club funded an excavation project — knocking the top off Pete and widening it. Volunteers recontoured the black diamond slope and decreased its grade. "It was a pleasure to watch the man's artistry with the bulldozer on Pete," remembers John Bruder, who then led the effort as ski club president.

1985: Rotary Charities grant funds and ski club member contributions paid for the construction of a barn for storing grooming and race equipment.

1985–1999: Recognizing that the hill could not fully depend on Mother Nature for its natural snow, in the 1980s, ski club leaders Trish Fiebing and Katy Hall led a charge to develop and raise money for Hickory's first snowmaking infrastructure. First added to Buck and Pete in 1985, snowmaking followed on Birch in 1999. The ski club also purchased four additional snow guns.

2007: The ski club initiated a $130,000 fundraising campaign, called "Snow on Swede," to expand the snowmaking infrastructure to Hickory's Swede trail. Completed in 2010, the program raised funds to pay for two additional snow guns, a new well pump and a high-tech booster station to move water more efficiently through the area. Local charities and community members contributed generously.

The parents and volunteers are what made it happen for us.

Valerie Hays Klein

GIVE A LITTLE, GET A LOT

Don Hicks was right: "If not for the volunteers, the ski club and high school racing would not exist." Sheer dedication from hundreds of volunteers made Hickory what it is today and turned novice athletes into mature skiers and racers with beautiful technique.

Although they donated their "time and hard work in often brutal conditions, when they could have been warm at home or having fun skiing themselves," ski club volunteers always took away much more than they gave. Paul Ameel believed that "the parents always had more fun than the kids" but also never forgot that "the races were for the kids."

The ski club, its volunteers and its racers all benefited. According to Carl Madion, "Skiing at Hickory taught my children and grandchildren commitment and discipline — how to treat other people. They had to learn to cope with disappointment and accept defeat."

Reflecting on the sport and her family's ski club experiences, Lorna Ameel agrees: "Skiing is the most wonderful thing. It's you. You have no excuses. The children's self-confidence is incredible — if they can race, they can do just about anything."

They were the course setters, the starters, the timers, the gatekeepers — they were the driving force.

Susan Elliott McGarry

A LABOR OF LOVE

For Dave Hicks and Gary Lambert, every Sunday morning during ski season — for twenty consecutive years — was the same. In the cold dark of winter, the two friends met at Big Boy for Southern omelets. Then they headed to Hickory. Known by hundreds of racers as simply "Hicks and Lambert," the men set courses and persnickety timing equipment for the Grand Traverse Ski Club's Sunday races.

Lugging spooled wire, Hicks and Lambert trudged up each face. Once there, they staked the starting area and then backed down the hill, unwinding and burying wire until they reached the finish gate. They set up each start gate and wired telephones for every course — a true labor of love. "It usually got down to crunch time, but we always managed," Hicks remembers. "Kids depended on it, and we never wanted to let them down."

By the time crowds arrived, the duo had clocked nearly five hours and consumed as many cups of coffee. They chatted while watching racers navigate their courses but always remained focused on potential equipment glitches. "All perfection," remembers Judy Hicks of her husband's demeanor those Sundays. "If there was a problem, he would devote himself to it until it got solved. He took it very seriously."

Hicks adds, "If the equipment didn't break down, we considered it a terribly successful Sunday. It was fun. It was a good challenge for us."

Hicks and Lambert would then gather and store all the equipment before heading home — sometimes a full two hours after Hickory had gone quiet. A common sight was Hicks slipping away with several broken telephones under his arm, returning the next Sunday with working ones.

Hicks, an engineer, became involved when his three children started racing in the early 1970s. Lambert jumped in just a few years later as his three sons began to race. Hicks and Lambert loved working

together as much as the work itself, and the duo's dedication outgrew their children. "It was always understood that we'd be back next year," Hicks recalls. "We kept it up because we were working together. We had so much fun. Gary was a fabulous guy. He'd do anything you asked of him with a smile on his face."

In 2000, a year after Lambert's death, Grand Traverse Ski Club President Matt Madion informed Hicks of a newly established annual award, the Hicks-Lambert Award, honoring the pair's years of volunteer service to the ski club. When asked how best to use the award, Hicks was clear: "Sportsmanship. When you think of an award, ability and being a champion come to mind. That's certainly important, but it was the sportsmanship of the skiers that amazed me. I saw the Grand Traverse Ski Club kids cheering for their competition. I thought that was pretty neat."

Awarded at the close of each ski season to one male and one female club racer elected by their peers for sportsmanship, the Hicks-Lambert Award is a true honor. Hicks tries to attend each ceremony so he can present the award personally and congratulate recipients: "I tell them this is a very meaningful award and that it shows me a lot about their character. I know Gary would say the same thing."

four: Pint-sized Club, Huge Improvements

five

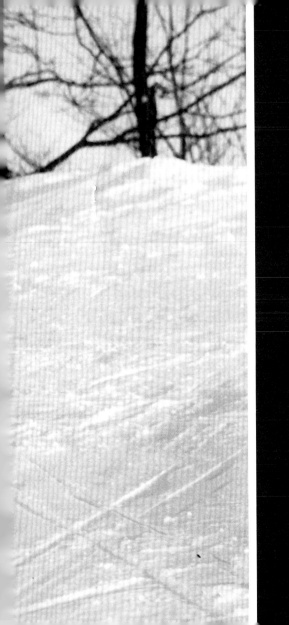

LITTLE RACERS, FULL SPEED

A LEGACY OF TOP RACERS

Aspen, Telluride, Bozeman, Lake Placid and Traverse City.

They have all been ranked top ski cities according to *Snow Country*, a national ski publication. Editors named the five communities and three others to its "Top Eight 'Mountain Town' School Districts" in 1993. Such news really wasn't new.

Thirty years earlier, Traverse City *Record-Eagle* Sports Editor Ken Bell noted in his sports column that "envious race officials…with equal natural facilities and larger populations are asking the same question: 'How does Traverse City do it?'" Those closest to the sport continue to credit small but mighty Hickory Hills and the Grand Traverse Ski Club's exceptional, comprehensive race programs.

"We don't have any more, or better, athletes than other communities," says Ed Johnson, head coach for the Traverse City West High School Alpine Ski Team and former St. Francis High School coach. "We basically have a training factory for ski racers by having Hickory right in town."

Lyn Salathiel, Traverse City Senior High School's coach from 1967 through 1985, credits success to the "farm team" model established by the ski club. The program prepares racers, starting as young as four, for the rigors of the sport.

Former Traverse City Senior High School racer Jon Elliott points to the skill and dedication of "the Grand Traverse Ski Club coaching staff, many of whom learned to ski at Hickory themselves and who return to Hickory year after year."

Everyone looks at the kids from Hickory as the ones to beat.

Denny Hoxsie

Others credit the steep vertical pitch of Pete. "Pete made more state championship skiers than any other hill," says Dave Hicks. "If they could make it down Pete, they had so much confidence. They could ski any slalom hill in the state."

Still others claim that Hickory's antiquated tow ropes require such upper-body strength that the racers become inherently tough. Whatever the reason, Hickory racers rank among the best in Michigan and in the nation.

IT'S OFFICIAL

When the Michigan High School Athletic Association (MHSAA) sanctioned high school ski racing in 1953, Traverse City Senior High School formed its first varsity ski team.

People are often surprised to learn that Trojan Hall of Fame Football Coach Jim Ooley coached the first ski team. Ooley "didn't know much about skiing, but he knew that hiking Pete would make us better athletes," remembers Larry Bensley. According to Bensley, the 1954 team captain, training on Pete paid off. That first season, two Hickory racers won individual championships at the first Lower Peninsula Championship at Sugar Loaf. Bensley won the men's downhill, and Barbara Sherberneau placed first in both the women's slalom and the women's downhill.

As the first varsity team sport for women in Traverse City, skiing drew daring young women to the sport. The first year, the Traverse City women's team proved itself by capturing the overall team championship title.

In 1955, Hickory Hills scored yet another first in Michigan high school sports: the first high school race held at night under lights was held at Hickory. The following year, Hickory hosted the Lower Peninsula Regional meet, which was the first championship ski meet held in Traverse City. Hosted by the ski club, the all-state competition included twelve teams competing in downhill and jumping events. A second high school championship meet was held at Hickory in 1963, again hosted by the Grand Traverse Ski Club. The Lower Peninsula Regional Championships returned to Hickory one final time in 1970.

During those early years, Traverse City's men and women dominated neighboring Michigan teams. But it wasn't all business. Marshall Carr remembers, "We traveled on a yellow school bus, both boys and girls teams together. The guys brought ukuleles, and we had sing-a-longs on every trip."

From 1954 to 1974, the MHSAA season culminated with the Lower Peninsula Regional Championships, known then as the "State" meet. In those years, Trojan women won fifteen titles, and St. Francis's women took two. The Trojan men earned twelve titles and the St. Francis men one. Over these two decades, six Traverse City women won individual championship titles: Barb Sherberneau, Joni Lovell, Sue Arnoldt, Francie Dorman, Val Hays and Cherie Gibson. Four men — Larry Bensley, John McGuffin, Lenny Ligon and Jerry Stanek — won individual championship titles.

Trojan Coach Lyn Salathicl remembers Hickory training "as the very best available anywhere. [Racers] could get in so many runs." They became physically fit — tougher than the competition — acting as manual groomers and packing snow by sidestepping across the hill. Carr recalls hiking uphill to strengthen his legs: "It packed the snow, which then lasted longer under hard skiing."

"Conditioning for the high school ski team in 1969 included boot-packing Pete and Buck — putting your ski boots on, then stomping your way up and down in close formation, then putting your skis on and doing it again," says Meredith Parsons McComb.

Susan Elliott McGarry agrees, recalling how power training continued: "Whether the tow ropes were working or not, we would walk up those hills, sidestepping to the Beach Boys' 'Barbara Ann.'"

In 1975, after the MHSAA sanctioned an official state championship meet, a new era of records began. Since then, Traverse City's high school teams combined have taken more state championship titles than any other community — nineteen for men and thirteen for women.

Despite their success, racers and coaches kept racing in perspective. As longtime Saint Francis Coach Pat Buron explains, "It's not about winning and losing but trying to make skiing a lifetime sport."

THE NERVE OF 10,000 BOYS

As a petite, spunky high schooler, Barbara Sherberneau, or "Bobbie" to her friends, loved sports. After her first swim team tryouts, however, the coaches suggested she take up knitting. Not a girl to be deterred, she learned to ski at Ci-Bo, and upon the 1952 inaugural opening of Hickory, she joined the Hickory Hills Ski Club as a ninth grader. Expertly coached by world-renowned skiers Peppi Teichner and Stein Eriksen, Sherberneau grew fierce and competitive, while her "graceful and elegant" style made her an immediate success and a joy to watch.

As the very first varsity sport offered to women at Traverse City Senior High School, downhill ski racing appealed to the risk taker in Sherberneau and other female mavericks. In 1954, just two years into skiing, Sherberneau became the first female high school state champion in both the downhill and slalom. Her stunning performance inspired women's athletic participation well before the enactment of Title IX.

Sherberneau's technique continued to improve under Teichner's and Eriksen's instruction. It was her spirit, though, that drove her to win. According to Coach Eriksen, Sherberneau had "the nerve of 10,000 boys." Peppi Teichner's daughter, Martha Teichner, remembers her as "a real prodigy of my father's. He was crazy about her. She was a tremendous competitor with character."

Sherberneau lived up to Eriksen's prediction that she would "go far in national competition." She placed runner-up in the 1954 Central United States Ski Association (CUSSA) Downhill Championship despite an "egg-beater spill" in fifty-five-mph winds and sleeting snow. Named to the CUSSA National Team in 1955, Sherberneau accomplished what many young women only dreamed of. One year later, Sherberneau returned home to coach her former team to yet another state championship at her home hill of Hickory. She was a darling of the media, and her image was chosen for several statewide marketing campaigns to promote Michigan ski resorts.

five: Little Racers, Full Speed   136

HICKORY RACERS HIT THE BIG TIME

Headquarters for the Central Division of the United States Ski Association (CUSSA) were first located in an office in downtown Traverse City, allowing for the development of close relationships early on with Traverse City skiers. Hickory trail honoree Jack Bensley served on the CUSSA board. Tom Joynt, a Grand Traverse Ski Club member and owner of the local Bilmar sports store, served as CUSSA's executive director. Traverse

City's Vojin Baic later assumed the role of the organization's national competition manager from 1966 until 1969, when the Central Division's headquarters relocated to Chicago.

With such close ties to the USSA's Central Division, Hickory hosted several CUSSA meets throughout the 1950s and 1960s, including the 1953 Central Division Championship. In 1961, Traverse City supplied more racers on the seven-state team than any other community in the Central Division.

Hickory breeds excellence. Throughout the decades, Hickory Hills and Grand Traverse Ski Club racers have earned national and international reputations. They've reached the podium at Junior Nationals. They have been named to Junior Olympic teams and to the U.S. Ski Team. They've skied in the World Cup, for top college teams and as professionals. Finally, they have served as race officials for USSA and International Ski Federation (FIS) races.

Any ski racer in Traverse City that was anything started skiing Sunday races through the Grand Traverse Ski Club at Hickory Hills.

Jerry Stanek

five: Little Racers, Full Speed

WHO'S JERRY STANEK?

1976 *Detroit Free Press* on Stanek's giant slalom win over Henri Duvillard

Most people know Jerry Stanek as a humble and unassuming cherry grower from Leelanau County. Most don't know him as a Traverse City legend. But that's what he is.

A champion racer, legendary ski coach and tireless volunteer, Stanek has continued to impact aspiring racers for nearly forty years thanks to his dedication, knowledge, technique, patience and caring.

At just five years old, Stanek learned to ski on Hickory's bunny. Albeit a slow start — staring at the tow rope for twenty minutes with his dad close at hand — the young Stanek finally grabbed hold. That grip is still tight: Stanek is passionate about skiing.

Stanek's racing career began at Hickory Hills and continued in high school when, from 1963 through 1966, he led his team to four Lower Peninsula championships. During his tenure there, he secured four perfect seasons, never losing a single meet. For three consecutive years, the *Detroit News* recognized Stanek with all-state honors. By that time, active in United States Ski Association (USSA), Stanek qualified for four Junior Nationals competitions.

After skiing for Fort Lewis College in Durango, Colorado, Stanek returned home to join his father and brother in the Stanek family business of cherry and apple farming. But he continued to race and make headlines. After Stanek's 1976 World Pro giant slalom win against international skier Henri Duvillard (an upset at the time), the *Detroit Free Press* sports page headline announced: "Stanek Stars in Holly's Ski 'Olympics.'"

With ski buddies Lenny Ligon and Sanford Blumenfeld, Stanek launched the first coaching organization for USSA racers in the Traverse City region in 1974. Stanek directed

five: Little Racers, Full Speed

the USSA program, with financial support from the Grand Traverse Ski Club, for fifteen years.

In 1979, Stanek and Don Dunsmore became assistant coaches to Traverse City's Senior High School Head Coach Lyn Salathiel. In addition to his coaching commitments, Stanek also became the director of the Grand Traverse Ski Club that same year. He held that position for five years until he and Don Dunsmore together assumed the head ski coach's role at Traverse City's Senior High School. Stanek remained dedicated to high school teams for more than twenty years, coaching varsity and junior varsity racers. He also coached Suttons Bay's high school team for three years and the Traverse City West High School team for three years.

Stanek and Dunsmore delivered ten state championships for Traverse City high schools, highlighted by eight consecutive boys' titles at Traverse City Central High School. After Dunsmore retired, Stanek enjoyed nine more state championships, including Traverse City West High School women's first-ever state championship in 2006. With that win, he became the first ski coach in Michigan to earn state championships from two different schools.

Stanek was inducted into the Michigan High School Ski Coaches Association's Hall of Fame, as well as the Grand Traverse Ski Club's Hall of Fame. During his tenure as a high school coach, he was named Michigan High School Coach of the Year several times.

Stanek's friend and coaching colleague Scott Winquist sums up Stanek's contribution to ski racing in Michigan: "His commitment to athletes, their parents and coaching our sport is beyond measure."

HICKORY'S GREAT RACERS

Hickory's progeny reads like a "who's who" list of northwest Michigan ski royalty.

Gregg Smith

LEN LIGON

Dubbed Traverse City's "top boy skier" by *Record-Eagle* Sports Editor Ken Bell, Len "Lenny" Ligon began his racing career under Hickory coaches Peppi Teichner and Ben Taylor. Considered reckless by some but admired by all, Ligon raced with determination and a continuous quest for speed. He analyzed his form and revised his technique until he found the fastest way down the hill: "Arms straight in front and all my weight forward."

Although too young to be eligible for a Junior Nationals race, Ligon qualified as a mere eighth grader. Old enough for eligibility just one year later, Ligon finished second in giant slalom at the 1961 Maine Junior Nationals. He held the distinction of placing top ten in that event for four years running. Ligon was named to the all-state team for four years during high school. Ligon later coached the St. Francis and Suttons Bay high school teams, as well as the Grand Traverse Ski Club's United States Ski Association team.

The fastest skier is not usually the best skier but the guy with the best head on his shoulders.

Lenny Ligon

five: Little Racers, Full Speed

TED LOCKWOOD

Coach Len Ligon remembers Ted Lockwood at Hickory: "He had lots of guts and went straight down the hill." While Lockwood's Hickory coaches taught him race technique, guts and straight lines clearly contributed to his 1976 downhill Central Division championship. Later that same year at the New Hampshire Junior Nationals, Lockwood took silver in the treacherous downhill, beating his way to the top from seventy-second place in the running order.

As a member of the U.S. Ski Team, Lockwood raced on the Can-Am, Nor-Am, Europa Cup and World Cup circuits. He retired from racing in 1981 with the 1980 Nor-Am overall championship under his belt. Lockwood went on to operate a junior race program and established Mt. Hood's second summer race camp. He has coached the Traverse City West High School team and hundreds of United States Ski Association and International Ski Federation (FIS) racers. As one of forty-nine U.S. licensed international technical delegates, Lockwood now officiates races throughout North America.

> Hickory Hills is one of the premier alpine training facilities for racers twelve years and under, in the Western Hemisphere, period.
>
> Ted Lockwood

150   five: Little Racers, Full Speed

TAMMY HAGERTY

Tammy Hagerty joined Hickory's Sunday racers at age five and fell in love with the sport. She honed her skills under Hickory's Austrian instructors, remembering the "international flair" they brought to Traverse City's small hill. Hagerty raced her way through high school and, as a twice-named all-state skier, contributed to Traverse City Senior High School's three-year streak as state champions. She won the individual giant slalom championship her senior year.

As a Middlebury College Ski Team member, Hagerty won both the St. Lawrence and Middlebury Carnival races in 1978. At the height of her racing career, she ranked among the top one hundred racers in the world based on her International Ski Federation (FIS) points. One of Hickory's top racers, Hagerty returned the gift of skiing to her community as a coach for the Grand Traverse and the Leelanau ski clubs.

> The volunteers are what make Hickory what it is.
>
> Tammy Hagerty

NICK NIXON

Nick Nixon still remembers buying his first Hickory season pass. He spent four dollars of his own money — a worthwhile investment for a little racer.

In high school, Nixon became the 1977 state champion in slalom and, one year later, earned a Junior Nationals championship. Nixon raced for the University of Colorado, winning his first collegiate slalom race as a freshman. From 1981 through 1983, he held the distinction of being ranked in the world's top ten based on his International Ski Federation (FIS) profile.

Racing opened the door to Nixon's professional career as a film and video producer. Spyder "discovered" Nixon in Boulder. He not only became the face of Spyder but also began to produce films for Spyder and other ski industry giants. Nixon continues to produce promotional video, television commercials and other ski films.

Hickory Hills supplied the platform for my success. The Grand Traverse Ski Club made it all possible with the Sunday races.

Nick Nixon

COLIN HALL

Colin Hall learned to ski at the age of five at Hickory's Record-Eagle Ski School. Hickory coaches Sandy Blumenfeld, Jerry Stanek and Lenny Ligon instilled in him a love for racing. In 1978 Hall entered Burke Mountain Academy in Vermont, where he could focus on skiing. Just three years later he was named to the U.S. Ski Team's development team. Based on his race points, he ranked among the top five in the nation for his age group. Hall returned to Traverse City in 1982 and coached Grand Traverse Ski Club CUSSA racers while also racing on the Central Division's MidAm circuit.

At the college level, Hall raced on Dartmouth's varsity ski team from 1983 to 1986, when his team won the Men's Alpine National Championship. After he graduated from Dartmouth, Hall turned to the sport of cycling and won several races in the United States, Canada, France and Belgium.

> I challenge you to find a place where kids can get more time on the snow than at Hickory Hills.
>
> Colin Hall

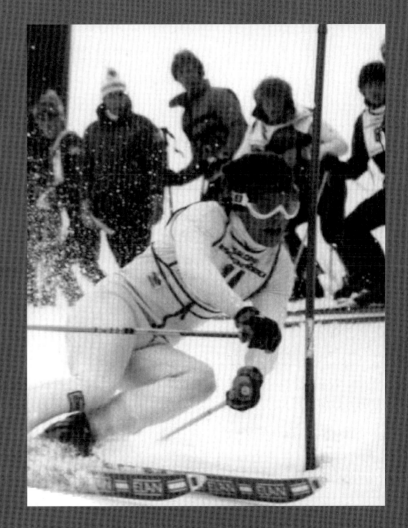

five: Little Racers, Full Speed

AUSTIN JOHNSON

Already skiing at the age of two and racing by age four, Austin Johnson grew up at Hickory. With years of Grand Traverse Ski Club clinics and races behind him, Johnson began racing with the United States Ski Association when he was ten years old. He quickly became a Junior Olympics star, earning nine podium finishes, including two golds and a J2 Nationals silver. A fourteen-year-old Johnson placed first in the Junior Olympics slalom, second in giant slalom and third in downhill. By sixteen, Johnson had earned his second-place ranking among the world's junior slalom racers. When he retired from amateur racing at the ripe age of twenty-one, Johnson had been a member of the National Development System for nine years.

Like many of the Hickory-bred champion racers, Johnson returned to Hickory and shared his skills and knowledge with young skiers by coaching at Traverse City's Central High School and the Grand Traverse Ski Club.

I would not have gotten to that level without Hickory. It was the prime place to start. You could go anywhere you wanted.

Austin Johnson

JENNIE VANWAGNER

Jennie VanWagner was only two when she started skiing at Hickory. She raced in the Grand Traverse Ski Club's Sunday races until she began racing with the United States Ski Association. VanWagner earned several Junior Olympic podiums, including a J2 Nationals downhill championship. One of six junior girls selected, VanWagner was named to the 2007 U.S. Development Team and the 2009 U.S. National World Junior Team.

VanWagner graduated from Utah's Rowmark Ski Academy. She returned home for her sophomore year of high school in 2003, however, and led Traverse City's Central High School to a state championship by sweeping both slalom and giant slalom events. VanWagner skied as a member of the University of Denver's 2010 national championship team. She also represented the United States and the University of Denver at the 2011 World University Games, where she prevailed in giant slalom.

Hickory played a huge role in my success.

Jennie VanWagner

five: Little Racers, Full Speed

HICKORY RACERS COME HOME

While their accomplishments as athletes are impressive, many of Hickory's great skiers also return to their home hill to coach and mentor young athletes. The list of racers turned Hickory coach is long: Barbara Sherberneau, Len Ligon, Jerry Stanek, Ted Lockwood, Austin Johnson, Tammy Hagerty, Jennie VanWagner, Mackenzie Bickel, Jeff Owens, Ellen Quirk, Ben Belyea, Abbey Rider, Tori Lockwood and many more.

Many Hickory racers also return to the ski club as board members, race officials, financial supporters and volunteers. The continuous dedication of those who have benefited from Hickory brings the founders' vision of volunteersim full circle and attests to the passion Hickory racers have for their sport.

six

FLEETING MOMENTS, LASTING MEMORIES

> My dad would only give us a ride one way up to Hickory. The other way we had to use our legs … and walk in our boots, carrying our skis all the way.
>
> Deb Tatch Julian

THE TREK TO THE HILL

Close to town and school, Hickory is an easy destination for young skiers. In the early years, desperate to get there, skiers employed various methods for the trek to the hill. The most popular — hitchhiking after school, skis and poles in hand and hopes held high. "I would stand on the side of the street with my skis. Someone would take me to the hill," recalls Ted Kramer, who caught rides more often than not.

The anticipation of heading downhill all the way home also made the trek up worthwhile. "My most vivid memory is skiing home at the end of a day at Hickory Hills," says Chuck Haberlein. "Over hill and dale, through the orchard, to my home on Monroe Street. It sure was fun!" In the early 1970s, Craig Fiebing hitchhiked to practice, and at the end of the night, he, too, headed down Swede onto Randolph Street all the way home.

For others, transportation to Hickory was trickier. "We walked from our house on Front and Elmwood with our skis, which got heavier and heavier as we walked," recalls Barbara Bjork Papazian. "It felt like a twenty-mile walk."

Jan Elliott Shugart enjoyed a more dramatic exit at the end of the night. "We often would watch for my parents' car to pull into the circular drive by the lodge and then bomb Pete all the way down, stopping just short of sliding under the car!"

Twenty-first-century skiers are more likely to be driven or bussed to the hill after school with either a few dollars in their pockets or a sack dinner, ready to ski until closing. Hickory's unique location is the key to it remaining a safe yet public ski hill over time — a pocket of open land protected from the encroachment of surrounding development.

six: Fleeting Moments, Lasting Memories

> You would wrap your fingers around the rope and squeeze, and when it finally grabbed or the splice came by, it would almost take your arm off.
>
> Lynn T. Rayle

THE ROPES

Though crucial to conditioning for any Hickory racer, the tow ropes and the racer have a love-hate relationship. The response of a nine-year-old skier at Hickory says it best: "The tow ropes help your arms get strong." While tow ropes are considered outdated, when it comes to competition, they mean might. Mike Quirk attributes his three daughters' podium finishes to Hickory's ropes, confirming the opinions of many coaches over the decades: the upper-body strength gained from tow rope use gives Hickory racers an advantage.

As Enrico Schaefer says of his three sons: "They refuse to ski anywhere else in Michigan. Chairlifts are for wimps. They're tow rope tough."

The memories shared by Hickory's old men and women of the hill have grown fonder over the years. "Heavy and fast," recalls Karen Strom of her mishaps. "My gloves iced up; I couldn't get a good grip. I began to slip back down the rope. … Others crashed into me or fell behind me, creating embarrassment and chaos."

Erin O'Connell remembers the frustration of leather tow rope guards: "After a time, they would mold to the shape of the rope itself, and our small hands would follow their contour and freeze into small crescents that could never gain purchase on the rope."

Once a skier could get a good grip, however, the sheer uphill exhilaration made the agony of the ropes worthwhile. "It was such a thrill going on the tow rope up alongside Ol' Pete," recalls Fitch Williams. "I didn't weigh much — it was a rush almost getting thrown up the hill."

Tow ropes are just one of Hickory's secrets to success and longevity. Riding the ropes is itself a source of power: "Not only does it give skiers significant training runs in a single practice," says Coach Ted Lockwood, "it also helps to build strength and balance."

I used to be lifted off the ground for a few feet.

Francie Dorman

> One year, curiosity claiming a rare victory over sanity, I tiptoed my skis to the top of Pete just to look down — and almost fell into the bay!
>
> Jack Lane

THE FACE OF PETE

Pete, Hickory's face. A source of fear, awe, achievement and pride, Pete is Hickory's central black diamond trail. Every skier who dares risk the short, steep plunge into the unknown knows Pete.

"Following a more or less terrifying tow rope ascent, all I could see was an incredibly steep slope and the lodge, way too close to the bottom of the hill," recalls Chuck Haberlein. "My only thought: 'If I don't stop in time, I'll go right through the ski racks, break into the lodge through the window and that'll be the end of me!'"

According to Cayce Weber, "Pete always scared the dickens out of the little kids."

Meredith Amon understands well the value of that fear: "How frightening could anything else in life be after you'd faced Pete?"

However scary the hill may be now with a grade of fifty degrees, Pete used to be even steeper. "The original natural fall line of Pete was extraordinary, because it got steeper as you went down the beast," recalls Bob Goddard. "It was never groomed, so to risk it was literally taking a plunge into the unknown. You had to navigate the nastiest, iciest bumps imaginable."

Hickory coaches have long respected the power of Pete in training and competition. Advanced skiers would shine on

That was a milestone — the Ol' Pete tuck.

Robert Tremp

On Pete, I'm at the edge of the world.

Gus Dutmers

Pete? It's tall and straight, and you have to stop in a hurry.

Clayton "Swede" Johnson

Pete, weaving through slalom gates, enjoying home-team advantage. "Opposing teams would pull into Hickory and think, 'This Podunk place,' until the course on Pete was set. Then they paid attention. We usually smoked them," recalls Jan Elliot Shugart.

Most racers, especially the young, always remember their first adventure on Pete. "I was scared." "I fell." "My legs were shaking." Whether sidestepping, scooting, snowplowing or tucking — a run on Pete remains a milestone for any Hickory skier.

six: Fleeting Moments, Lasting Memories

THE LODGE

Don't be fooled by the simplicity. Warm, easygoing, relaxed but rustic – the lodge is Hickory's heart, unchanged. "I like that they haven't changed it," says one nine-year-old. "The lodge has a big fire; it's nice and cozy."

Local architect Orus Eash designed Hickory's original twenty-three-by-sixty-four-foot lodge. Decades later, Hickory's warming lodge remains a place where kids are known by name, where it's safe to leave unlocked bags and belongings and where children and adults are bound to find friends and food to refuel. An open fireplace and the smell of burning wood warm the small interior — a shelter with an alpine sensibility, safe and warm during cold winter days and nights. Francie Dorman holds fond memories of the lodge: "The roaring fireplace, the joy of sitting around the fire with my friends while melting frozen mittens, will never be forgotten."

As if remembering last night's meal, Hickory skiers still recall the snack bar. "It was operated by Jo Adams. We were her kids," says Dick Swan. "She was vibrant, positive, a mother figure for us. Come to think of it, I have never had a better burger since."

Mike Harris recalls when burgers at the lodge were just twenty-five cents, affordable even for a young skier with some pocket change. Back then, skiers could simply charge their burgers and hot dogs to their family's tab.

Mike Quirk remembers fondly concession operator Pete Bentley: "He was wonderful; if you couldn't afford a hot dog, he'd give it to you. Everybody loved him."

The pride of Hickory's founders was built into the foundation of the lodge. Talk to any Hickory skier and the lodge will feature prominently in the experience. It embodies more than just food and shelter, and it holds more than the pride of a bygone era. "The welcoming, comfortable lodge, the smell of melting mittens on the woodstove, the caring curmudgeon at the snack bar" — Jan Elliott Shugart knows the lodge is where memories have been made.

> Money did not matter at Hickory or what your parents did for a living. What mattered most was your jump-making abilities and teamwork.
>
> Collin Salisbury

SHENANIGANS

Deposit a rowdy group of preteens without parents? Antics. Mischief. Preteens on skis? Naughty. Over the years, city employees, bound and determined to put a stop to less acceptable shenanigans, have halted some little skiers in their tracks. But, they haven't caught them all. Building jumps. Stretching, swinging and snapping ropes. Bombing hills and hotdogging. They are all just as much of the Hickory experience as conquering Pete.

"We were like a mini-Marine recon unit using our skills of subterfuge to foil the likes of Mr. Bernie Fleetwood and his enforcement of the 'no jump making policy,'" recalls Collin Salisbury. "Bernie was a worthy adversary, and though we tried to subvert his authority often, we had immense respect for him."

Fitch Williams now admits, "We were awful ski brats sometimes. We'd snap the rope, trying to knock the guy off behind us when we unloaded at the top. The target would let go and grab after the whip went by, but some hapless young adult on his first trip would get flipped clear off the rope."

Warren Miller kicking back with Grand Traverse Ski Club racers, 1958.

I was kicked out of Hickory more than anyone, harmless activities from building jumps over Buck's tow rope and off the building to setting off stink bombs in the lodge.

Sam Porter

six: Fleeting Moments, Lasting Memories   177

BROKEN SKIS, BROKEN BONES

Although economical and widely popular, the 1950s-era hickory skis were heavy and long. Lace-up leather boots kept the cold in, not out. Wool coats and knitted mittens provided little protection from subzero temperatures and fast-moving tow ropes. Rudimentary gear in the early days led to cold fingers, cold feet and broken bones.

In the 1950s and 1960s, before the advent of impact-release bindings, injuries were almost expected, and Hickory had its fair share. Mary Wagamon remembers the Hickory Hills Hall of Fame "for broken legs," and in 1953, she joined the injury club. Karen Bjork Strom recalls broken equipment regularly displayed in the lodge with pride.

But not every skier enjoyed such attention. "I broke my first pair of skis on the bunny slope at the age of five," remembers Gary Keyes. "They wanted to put them with the other skis over by the windows, with kids' names on them, but I was too embarrassed. I skied home on one ski."

six: Fleeting Moments, Lasting Memories   179

I have lots of memories sitting on the bench putting on and taking off my ski boots, the old-fashioned ones with two or three sets of laces. I still remember drinking hot chocolate and wondering if I should just pour it on my cold feet.

Fitch Williams

ROMANCE

Shenanigans give way to romance. Memories of first kisses at night with snow sparkling under the lights along Jack's Trail — Hickory's most popular smooching spot — mingle with the intangible magic of skiing.

Night skiing under the lights, while novel in the 1950s, is expected in the twenty-first century. But the contrast between the light and the dark, the reflection of the snow on the slopes, the shadows on the terrain and the sheer delight of being outside on a cold, dark midwinter night when others are already tucked in — all make for a particular ambiance understood only by those who have experienced it. As Larry Bensley says: "It was romantic." It still is.

The sound of the skis crunching in the snow, the rope running and the tranquility of being alone out there — it was always romantic.

Rosie Hutchison

six: Fleeting Moments, Lasting Memories

> Long skis with no edges, bamboo poles, first kiss! A marvelous experience!
>
> Mary Wagamon

"When I hear 'Hickory Hills,' memories of firsts become the dominant images in my mind," says Collin Salisbury. "First falls, first jumps, first kisses, first full moons."

Sally Woodward describes Hickory simply as a "magical place with good friendships and wonderful times." And for some, Hickory's romance was more than just a teenage fling. Sandy Blumenfeld, a Hickory coach and volunteer, held his wedding reception in the lodge. Will Moss, a Grand Traverse Ski Club coach, proposed to Coach Lauren White on Christmas Day by writing in the snow on the face of Pete "Will you marry me?"

NARROW LENS, WIDE VIEW

An athlete and civic leader, Jack Bensley pursued another passion late into his life — photography. He excelled as an amateur photographer at a young age. In high school, his photographs won top honors in a national contest hosted by the American Institute of the City of New York. As he matured, his talent and focus evolved. An amateur with the skill of a professional, Bensley processed and printed all his own work in a home darkroom. He paid meticulous attention to detail, documenting all his negatives and prints in chronological order and outlining each photo's subject matter.

Bensley took a keen interest in the local area, Hickory Hills being a favorite subject. He never left home without his camera and whenever he was at Hickory had camera in hand. Bensley's love of ski racing gave him incentive to chronicle decades worth of Hickory's races, including high school and regional races. Astute with a natural eye, he recorded Hickory's development, landscape, racers and volunteers.

Bensley's family provided the authors with access to his collection. While poring over these photos, the authors' vision for *Light the Night* crystalized. The photos themselves told the story; the authors simply needed to articulate it. Bensley's meticulous approach to his craft, work ethic and life view allow us to see Hickory as it was in the 1950s and 1960s — through the eyes of Hickory's earliest skiers. The generosity of the Bensley family in permitting the publication of Bensley's photos made this view possible.

Bensley's generosity of spirit not only made his photos come to life but also had a significant impact on others. According to his younger brother, Larry, "Jack really cared about other people. He always gave his photos away to kids and parents for them to enjoy."

He's still giving them away.

THE MAGIC OF LIGHTED SLOPES

Hickory has stayed the same: the cold, brisk air; the scrape of skis as you try to stop at the bottom; the fast tow ropes and the magic of the lighted slopes. Memories of a lifetime.

Karen Strom, a Hickory skier in the 1950s

ACKNOWLEDGEMENTS

We are indebted to the Bensley family for sharing their family archives, photographs and home movies. This story could not have been told without their gracious and enthusiastic support.

To Loraine Anderson and the *Record-Eagle*, thank you for your early support of the project and creating a blog site, "Do You Have a Hickory Hills Story?" to collect stories and memories. To those who shared their personal experiences with us through interviews, e-mails and blog responses, we hope we have done your stories justice.

Special thanks to Nick Edson of Cherryland Electric Cooperative for his advice, enthusiasm, encouragement and faith in us.

Thank you to our partners, the city of Traverse City and the Grand Traverse Ski Club for their invaluable support.

For their hard work, dedication and guidance, we would like to thank our advisory board members, Larry Bensley, Bill Thomas, Gregg Smith, Annie Devries, Trish Fiebing and Matt Madion. Your wisdom and enthusiasm made us work even harder.

We appreciated the assistance of the staff of Traverse Area Public Schools, including Carrie Inglis, Pat Mericle, Charles Rennie, Courtney Mazurek, Karyn Hertel and Carol Roehrich. Thanks too to Ellen King and the staff of the Michigan Community Service Commission. Our participation on Michigan's Service Learning Youth Council was invaluable.

We also would like to express our gratitude to those whose work was instrumental in this publication: Tarra Dalley Warnes, Nikki Stahl, Deb Hawkins, Jonathan Stein, Jerry Stanek, Sandy Blumenfeld, and Charity Madion.

For their early support of the project, we thank the History Center of Traverse City and archivist Peg Siciliano for in-kind support. We also would like to recognize Tom West and the U.S. Ski and Snowboard Hall of Fame for graciously allowing us to conduct research in its library.

Thank you to our moms. We could not have done this without them.

SOURCES

CONTRIBUTORS

Dawn Shipman Abraham, Lorna Ameel, Meredith Raftshol Amon, Vojin Baic, Phil Balyeat, Fran Batsakis, Larry Bensley, Tom Bensley, Sandy Blumenfeld, Gil Bogley, John Bruder, Pat Buron, Marshall Carr, Jesse Clem, Pam Couturier Collins, Bob Core, Francie Dorman, Nick Edson, Jan Elliott, Joe Elliott, Jon Elliott, Max Elliott, Robert Fifarek, Bernie Fleetwood, Bob Goddard, Meg Wilson Godfrey, Lisa Oddy Grace, David Greene, Ken Gregory, Peter Haase, Chuck Haberlein, Tammy Hagerty, Colin Hall, Mike Harris, Mary Hazelton, Paul Hazelton, Dave Hicks, Denny Hoxsie, Mary Huhnsberger, Rosie White Hutchinson, Austin Johnson, Clayton Johnson, Ed Johnson Jr., Ed Johnson Sr., Deb Tatch Julian, Gary Keyes, Jack Keyes, Robert Kirschlager, Valerie Hays Klein, Ron Korn, Ted Kramer, Craig Kreiser, Jack Lane, Julie Lane Leep, Len Ligon, Ted Lockwood, Kelley Long, Barbara Sherberneau Loveland, Chris MacInnes, Carl Madion, Edward Mann, Bob McCall, Mac McClelland, Meredith Parsons McComb, Susan Elliott McGarry, Dan McGee, John McMillan, Bev Merchant, Allison Merrill, Helen Milliken, Gail Sherk Mitchell, Lauren Moss, Will Moss, Claire Nixon, Nick Nixon, Erin O'Connell, Jeff Owens, Roger Popa, Sam Porter, Mike Quirk, Lynn Rayle, Karen Eitzen Rennie, Pete Rennie, Lyn Salathiel, Collin Salisbury, Enrico Schaefer, Howard Schweitzer, Abbie Sirrine, Barry Smith, Gregg Smith, Pat Smith, Jerry Stanek, Karen Strom, Pete Strom, Dick Swan, Martha Teichner, Deb Merchant Thomack, Christopher Tobias, Rob Tremp, Jennie VanWagner, Lauren Vaughn, Mary Wagamon, Cayce Weber, Tom West, Paul Wiley, Beth Williams, Fitch Williams, Sharalee Wilson, Scott Winquist, Kathy Woods, Sally Woodward

WORKS CITED

Antczak, Joe. "Competititve Prep Skiing New Rage of Northland." *The Grand Rapids Press*, January 21, 1962, sec. C.

Bensley Family. Various family correspondence, photos and documentation. Traverse City, Michigan.

Beukema, C. H. "West Michigan Adds Two Winter Sports Centers." *Chicago Tribune,* December 7, 1952.

Cheers: A History of Trojan High School Sports. Traverse City Central High School Sports Publishing Class, 1998.

City of Traverse City. Various public records. Accessed at City of Traverse City offices.

Erickson, Howard. "Stanek Stars in Holly's Ski 'Olympics.'" *The Detroit Free Press,* February 1976.

Fry, John. *The Story of Modern Skiing.* University Press of New England, 2006.

Garfield Township. Various public records. Accessed at Garfield Township offices.

Gould, Pat. "The Middle West Is Ski-Minded." *The New York Times,* December 7, 1947.

Grand Traverse Ski Club. Various club reports and minutes, 1953–2010.

Kircher, Molly. *Boyne (People History Memories).* Boyne Resorts, 2008

Leelanau Enterprise. "Winter Sports Took Hold in 1940s." February 18, 2010. Accessed at http://www.leelanaunews.com.

Legacy: Austria's Influence on American Skiing. Culture Films LLC. DVD, 2006.

Michigan High School Athletic Association. Various public records. Accessed at http://www.mhsaa.com.

The Michigan Skier. Various news clips, photos and advertisements, 1954–1955. Accessed at United States Ski Hall of Fame and Museum, Ishpeming, Michigan, May 2010.

The Mid-West Skier. Various news clips, photos and advertisements, 1956–1957. Accessed at United States Ski Hall of Fame and Museum, Ishpeming, Michigan, May 2010.

Page, Eleanor. "Michigan Hill Gaining Fame as Ski Center." *Chicago Tribune,* December 28, 1947.

Terrell, Mike. "The Story Behind the Hills." *Reflections by the Bays.* Traverse City Record-Eagle, Winter 2010.

Traverse Area Chamber of Commerce. Various public records and documentation. Traverse City, Michigan, June 2011.

Traverse City Central High School. Yearbook records. Traverse City, Michigan.

Traverse City Record Eagle. Various news articles, photos and stories, 1950–2010. Accessed at Northwestern Michigan College.

Traverse City Saint Francis High School. Yearbook records. Traverse City, Michigan.

Traverse City West High School. Yearbook records. Traverse City, Michigan.

United States Ski Hall of Fame. Various public records, photos, exhibits and documentation. Accessed at United States Ski Hall of Fame and Museum, Ishpeming, Michigan, May 2010.

Winter Wonderland. Produced and directed by William Jamerson. DVD, 1995.

DONORS

Thank you to all of our donors, who believed in this project and supported us. Your gifts allowed one hundred percent of the book's proceeds to be donated to Preserve Hickory, a nonprofit organization created to preserve this special place in our community.

We are especially grateful to the following local, philanthropic leaders who made significant donations to support the publication of *Light the Night*.

The Les and Anne Biederman Foundation
Cherryland Electric Cooperative
The Huntington National Bank
Oleson Foundation
The Rotary Good Works Fund

HICKORY'S STATE CHAMPIONS

MICHIGAN HIGH SCHOOL ATHLETIC ASSOCIATION STATE FINALS 1975-PRESENT

YEAR	NAME	EVENT
1975	Judy Kramer	Slalom
1976	Tammy Hagerty	Giant Slalom
1977	Nick Nixon	Slalom
1979	Dan Lautner	Slalom, Giant Slalom
1980	Dan Lautner	Slalom, Giant Slalom
1983	Kathy Skendzel	Giant Slalom
1985	Jim Woodburne	Slalom
1986	Jim Woodburne	Slalom
1990	Heather Johnson	Giant Slalom
1993	Ben Elkins	Slalom
1995	Mike Mohrhardt	Slalom
1995	Nate Smith	Giant Slalom
1996	Ellen Quirk	Slalom, Giant Slalom
1997	Marin Schulz	Giant Slalom
1997	Brooke Schulz	Slalom
1998	Mackenzie Bickel	Giant Slalom
1999	Brooke Schulz	Slalom, Giant Slalom
1999	Ben Belyea	Slalom, Giant Slalom
2000	Nate Elhart	Giant Slalom
2000	Mackenzie Bickel	Giant Slalom
2000	Liz VanWagner	Slalom
2005	Jennie VanWagner	Slalom, Giant Slalom
2006	Abbey Rider	Slalom
2008	Madison McLachlan	Slalom
2009	Madison McLachlan	Giant Slalom
2009	Tori Lockwood	Slalom

PHOTO CREDITS AND IDENTIFICATION*

*All photographs are courtesy of the Bensley Family with the exception of those noted in parentheses.

COVER
Hickory under lights, c. 1955.

MIND, BODY AND SOUL
x. The view from inside Hickory's lodge, c. 1954.

FOREWORD
xiv. Martha Teichner crosses the finish line while Wayne Cowell, Len Ligon and Max Wysong record her time, c.1955. **xvi.** Peppi Teichner and his daughter Martha Teichner, c. 1955.

INTRODUCTION
xviii. View of Hickory Hills from the top of Birch, c. 1955.

CHAPTER ONE HUMBLE HILL, BIG VISION
xxii. Hickory Hills from the top of Buck, c. 1952. **2.** Two skiers on Swede, c. 1953. **3.** Loren Bensley at Ci-Bo Hill, 1950. **5.** Ci-Bo was located just south of the intersection of Division Street and 14th Street on the east side of the highway, 1950. (Record-Eagle) **6.** Ci-Bo Hill, 1950. (Record-Eagle) **7** Ci-Bo Hill, 1950. (Record-Eagle) **8.** Loren Bensley in front of Hickory's lodge, c. 1952. **10.** John Norton, Orus Eash, Loren Bensley, Gerald "Buck" Williams, Glenn Loomis, c. 1951. **10.** Buck Williams and unknown identity, 1951. **12.** Community volunteers and city workers at Hickory, 1951. **13.** Architect's rendering of Hickory Hills Lodge, c. 1951. (Record-Eagle) **13.** Building Hickory's fireplace, 1951. **14.** Oscar "Swede" Johnson, c. 1951. **15.** Loren Bensley, Lud Garthe, Buck Williams, John Norton, 1961. **16.** Lodge at night, c. 1955. **17.** Tow rope construction. c. 1951. **18.** Geraldine Cowell, c. 1953. **20.** Sonja Garthe, Claudette Kirby, Karen Schubert, c. 1953. **21.** Len Ligon, Marilyn Ligon and family, c. 1953. **23.** Hickory's trail map, c. 2000. (City of Traverse City) **24.** Hickory trail signs **25.** Hickory trail signs **27-29.** Hickory improvements, 1957-1959 **30.** Aerial view of Hickory, c. 1955. **32.** Land map of Hickory Hills, c. 2010. (Brian Vandenbrand, Garfield Town-

ship) **34.** Entry improvement, c. 1957. **35.** Development of Swede, c. 1956. **36.** Roy and Ellen Brigman, c. 1953. (Kathy Woods) **37.** "Handicampers" in front of Hickory's lodge, c. 1953. (Kathy Woods) **38.** Physicians examine campers in Hickory's lodge, c. 1953. (Kathy Woods) **40-41.** Camp Roy-El "Handicampers" at Hickory Hills, c. 1953. (Kathy Woods)

CHAPTER TWO EMERGING SPORT, LEGENDARY LEADER
42. Robert Gresham (#33) of The Leelanau School. Lower Peninsula Regional Championship jump competition at Hickory, 1956. **45.** Peppi Teichner presents a young skier with a Record-Eagle Ski School patch, c. 1954. **48.** Peppi Teichner and Larry Bensley, c. 1953. **51.** Peppi Teichner, c. 1953.

CHAPTER THREE SMALL TOWN, BIG WORLD
52. Pete and Buck from Birch, c. 1955. **55.** The tow path to Hickory's "Intermediate" trail, originally located between Buck and Bunny (abandoned), c. 1953 **56.** Hickory's original bunny hill (now lower Birch), c. 1952. **58.** Record-Eagle Ski School patch, c. 1955. **59.** Peppi Teichner (5th from left) and the Record-Eagle Ski School instructors, c. 1951. **60.** Record-Eagle Ski School instructors: Don Orr, Jerry Meach, Russ Adams, Peppi Teichner, Larry Bensley, Marilyn Ligon, Joey Cowell, Helen Milliken, Ann Price, c. 1952. (Record-Eagle) **61.** Record-Eagle Ski School demonstration at Hickory, c. 1952. **63.** Stein Eriksen demonstrates his technique at Hickory, c. 1955. **64.** Stein and Tom Bensley, c. 1955. **64.** Stein and Boyne instructors in Hickory's lodge, c. 1955. **64.** Stein lacing up his leather boots in front of Hickory's fireplace, c. 1955. **65.** Stein and Boyne instructors at Hickory's snack bar with Jo Adams, c. 1955. **66.** Spectators watch Stein Eriksen demonstrate his reverse shoulder technique at Hickory Hills, c. 1955. **68.** Kiwanis Ski School patch, c. 1975. **69.** Kiwanis Ski School members in Kiwanis K formation on the base of Buck, c. 1965. **69.** Royce Asher, Hickory's Head Ski Professional, c. 1955. **70.** Ski School Sponsors Honored: Curt Alward, general manager of J.W. Milliken, Inc., department store; Bill Smith, editor of the Record-Eagle; Bud King, President of the Grand Traverse Ski Club and Paul Hazelton, chairman of the Traverse City Kiwanis Club, February 12, 1962. (Record-Eagle) **75.** Original Hickory Hills season patches **76.** Tom Bensley, Max Wysong, Jim Merrill, Mike Orr, Dave Merrill, c. 1960. **78.** Don Orr Ski Shop, c. 1960. **79.** Don Orr Ski Shop, c. 1960. **81.** Vojin Baic. (Baic Family) **82.** Vojin Baic. (Baic Family)

CHAPTER FOUR PINT-SIZED CLUB, HUGE IMPROVEMENTS
84. Max Wysong and Jack Merrill check the clock as a racer crosses the finish, c. 1955. **86.** Sunday race at Hickory Hills, c. 1955. **87.** Larry Bensley racing down Buck, c. 1954. **89.** Jack Merrill, c. 1953. **90.** Ski Patrol demonstration on Buck: c. 1953. **91.** Jack Merrill Ski Patrol Room. **93.** Roy Ryerson (middle) and members of Hickory's Ski Patrol, c. 1955. **94.** Sunday race at Hickory, c. 1958. **94.** Marilyn and Pete Rennie watch a Sunday race at Hickory, c. 1958. **96.** Grand Traverse Ski Club volunteers hauling equipment at a club-sponsored race, Mt. Holiday. Left to right: identity unknown, Glenn Hazelton, Ken Lindsay Jr. **97.** Grand Traverse Ski Club volunteers hauling equipment at a club-sponsored race, Mt. Holiday. Left to right: Dale Wares, identity unknown, Len Ligon Sr., Ken Lindsay Sr. **98.** Racer Tom Hall, c. 1955. **99.** Grand Traverse Ski Club volunteers and racers, c. 1953. Left to right: Max Wysong, Mike Merrill, Mickey Joynt. **99.** View of finish from lodge, c. 1955. **100.** Grand Traverse Ski Club volunteers and timing toboggan. Left to right: Keith Hazelton, Paul Ameel and Dick Babel. **101.** Racer crosses finish, c. 1955. **102.** Grand Traverse Ski Club racer presented with a ribbon, c. 1955. **102.** Grand Traverse Ski Club racers and their ribbons, c. 1955. **102.** Grand Traverse Ski Club racers show off their hardware, c. 1955. **104.** Jerry Stanek, Dave Kipley, Len Ligon, Dave Merrill, Jim Merrill at top of Buck, c. 1955. **107.** High School race at Hickory Hills, c. 1960. **110.** Hickory manager Bernie Fleetwood maintains Pete, c. 1981. Record-Eagle. **114.** Grand Traverse Ski Club racers and volunteers gather at the bottom of Buck, c. 1955. **114.** Grand Traverse Ski Club volunteers, Gordon Cornwell and Len Ligon Sr. **116.** Grand Traverse Ski Club racers and volunteers and the start. **116.** Traverse City High School racers and coach at the start, Len Ligon, Russ Luttinen, Lorna Stulen, c. 1960. **117.** Grand Traverse Ski Club course volunteers, Wayne Cowell and Dell Zimmerman, c. 1955. **118.** Jack Bensley encourages his son Tom at the start, c. 1961. **119.** Grand Traverse Ski Club parent at leaderboard, c. 1955. **121.** Dave Hicks and Gary Lambert setting up for a Sunday race. (Hicks) **123.** Gary Lambert and Dave Hicks. (Hicks)

CHAPTER FIVE LITTLE RACERS, FULL SPEED

124. Traverse City High School racers at the top of Buck, c. 1960. Left to Right: Ken Lindsay, Len Ligon and Bonnie Stultz. (Sandy Blumenfeld) **127.** High School racers at Hickory practice, c. 1965. Left to right: Ted Thirlby, Tom Shield, Tom Bensley and Mack Beers. **128.** Traverse City High School racers and Coach Jim Ooley in front of lodge, c. 1954. Left to right: Russ Adams, Jerry Meach, Larry Bensley, Coach Ooley, John McGuffin. **130.** Traverse City High School championship team, Left to right: Coach Jim Ooley, Mary Weller, John McGuffin, Joey Cowell, Jerry Meach, Pat Rankin, Ted Lemon, Russ Adams. Front row: Larry Bensley and Barbara Sherberneau, c. 1954 **133.** Traverse City High School racers: Roy Arnold, Jim Beebe, John McGuffin, Russ Adams, Jerry Meach, Joey Cowell, Joan Lovell, Meredith Raftshol, Sue Gregory, c. 1956. **135.** Barbara Sherberneau at Hickory, c. 1954. **136.** Barbara Sherberneau, Coach Stein Eriksen and Larry Bensley, c. 1955. **137.** Barbara Sherberneau and Sue Cowell, c. 1954. **138.** 1961 Central Division Championship team members. Left to right top row: Ken Lindsay, Ken King, Len Ligon, Dave Merrill, Jim Olsen. Left to right bottom row: Val Hays, Cherie Gibson, Lorna Stulen, Bonnie Stultz, Jane Frazier. **138.** Hickory skier Mickey Joynt, c. 1958. **139.** Mike Merrill, c. 1961 **141.** 1961 Central Division team members. Left to right top row: Ken Lindsay, Ken King, Len Ligon, Dave Merrill, Jim Olsen. Left to right bottom row: Cherie Gibson, Lorna Stulen, Val Hays, Bonnie Stultz, Jane Frazier. **143.** Jerry Stanek tears up the course at Boyne Mountain, c. 1970. (Stanek) **143.** Jerry Stanek at the start, c. 1970. (Stanek) **144.** Coach Jerry Stanek with high school racer, c. 1995. (Record-Eagle) **146.** Starter Paul Ameel lining up racers, c. 1960. **149.** Len Ligon, 1961. **150.** Ted Lockwood, U.S. Nationals at Squaw Valley, 1977. (Lockwood) **151.** Tammy Hagerty, c. 1976. (Record-Eagle) **152.** Nick Nixon, University of Colorado race, c. 1980. (Nixon) **153.** Colin Hall: Mid-Am Giant Slalom at Iron Mountain, 1983 (Hall) **154.** Austin Johnson at Aleyska, Alaska, 1997. (Johnson) **155.** Jennie VanWagner (VanWagner) **156.** The lodge, c. 1955.

CHAPTER SIX FLEETING MOMENTS, LASTING MEMORIES

158. Fun on Pete, c. 1955. **160.** Jim Merrill and Tom Bensley trekking to Hickory, c. 1955. **163.** Buck tow rope, c. 1955. **164.** Moguls on Pete, c. 1955. **166.** High School racers face Pete, c. 1960. **167.** Mogul skiers on Pete, c. 1955. **168.** Hickory's lodge **168.** The fireplace in Hickory's lodge, c. 1954. (Stanek) **170.** Hickory's lodge at night, c. 1955. **172.** Jo Adams behind Hickory's snack bar, c. 1955. **173.** Inside Hickory's lodge, c. 1954. **175.** Dick Swan, Mickey Joynt, Mike Merrill catching air, c. 1959. **176.** Warren Miller and Grand Traverse Ski Club skiers, Tom Bensley, Dave Merrill and Jack Bickler, c. 1958. **177.** Skiers enjoy Buck, c. 1955. **179.** Injured skiers, Harvey Calcutt and Tom Bensley show off hardware in front of lodge. **181.** Dave Merrill, unknown identity, Tom Bensley, Jack Bickler, c. 1960. **183.** Atop Hickory Hills, c. 1958. **184.** Lovebirds Larry Bensley and Joey Cowell, c. 1954. **185.** Proposal on Pete, c. 2009. (Lauren and Will Moss)

NARROW LENS, WIDE VIEW

187. Jack Bensley and Mike Merrill, c. 1960. (Record-Eagle)
187. Jack Bensley

THE MAGIC OF LIGHTED SLOPES

189. View of Hickory at night from Birch, c. 1955.

THE AUTHORS

Molly Tompkins was born in London, England, and lived in Seattle until the age of eleven, when she moved to Traverse City. She didn't really learn to ski until she donned a pair of used skis and headed up to Hickory Hills. She loves the sport. Like her extended family, she shares fond memories of racing at Hickory and still enjoys getting out on the rope tows and under the lights. Molly was the proud recipient of the Grand Traverse Ski Club's Hicks-Lambert Sportsmanship award. She is a senior at Traverse City Central High School, where she is the governor of Student Senate and participates in cross-country, debate and track.

Ryan Ness was born in Evanston, Illinois, and moved to Traverse City at the age of five. A few days after learning to ski, Ryan entered his first Sunday race at Hickory, and his love for the sport was born. Ryan was a member of the Central Division's Junior Olympic Team in 2006, 2007 and 2008. As a member of the varsity ski team at Traverse City West High School, Ryan achieved MHSAA all-state honors. The regional champion in slalom in 2011, he was named cocaptain of the *Record-Eagle's* All-Region Dream Team. Ryan's favorite winter nights are spent under the lights at Hickory.

Based on their community service project, both Molly and Ryan were invited to serve as members of the Michigan Service Learning Youth Council. They attended two retreats in Lansing and worked with two dozen other Michigan students with passions for community service. Collaborating with these students helped shape the authors' vision for *Light the Night*.